PENGUIN BOOKS

GET UNSTUCK

Mae Kwan is a wellness creative who helps people break free from limiting patterns and step into their authentic power. Originally trained as an architect in London, she established her interior design business and a fashion accessories label after moving to Hong Kong, where she also began studying *Vedanta* with her mentor—a relationship that continues to deepen her spiritual practice today.

Mae's life took a pivotal turn when she relocated to Singapore in 2015 and transitioned into the wellness industry. Certified in Tibetan Singing Bowl healing, Emotional Freedom Technique, and Feng Shui design, along with being a trained yoga instructor who has also studied BodyTalk and Mindscape, Mae brings an intuitive approach to her work, creatively blending different modalities including meditation to meet each client's unique needs.

In 2022, Mae created UNSTUCK™, a transformational framework that has become the cornerstone of her practice. Through workshops, speaking engagements, and immersive experiences, she uses this method to guide individuals and teams from survival mode into creative flow, helping them heal past wounds, restore balance, and unlock their full potential.

Mae uses emotions as a roadmap for transformation, helping clients connect the dots between their limiting beliefs, old narratives, and behavioural patterns to create profound shifts that ripple through every aspect of their lives. Her work centres on a simple yet powerful belief: that by honouring our emotions and inner wisdom, we can unravel the stories that keep us stuck and create lives that truly reflect who we are meant to be.

ADVANCE PRAISE FOR *GET UNSTUCK*

'Authentic human connection soothes our nervous system and as such is a vital component to getting un-stuck. Mae Kwan provides this and a myriad of other tools to help you re-centre and thrive amidst the chaos of our world.'

—Simone Heng, award-winning
author of *Let's Talk About Loneliness*

Get Unstuck

The Road to Freedom

Mae Kwan

PENGUIN BOOKS
An imprint of Penguin Random House

PENGUIN BOOKS

Penguin Books is an imprint of the Penguin Random House group of companies whose addresses can be found at global.penguinrandomhouse.com

Published by Penguin Random House SEA Pte Ltd
40 Penjuru Lane, #03-12, Block 2
Singapore 609216

Penguin Random House SEA

First published in Penguin Books by Penguin Random House SEA 2026

10 9 8 7 6 5 4 3 2 1

ISBN 9789815362411

Typeset in Adobe Garamond Pro, EB Garamond by MAP Systems, Bangalore, India

www.penguin.sg

Contents

Preface

Getting Unstuck

UNSTUCK is a wellness programme based on my personal healing and spiritual journey. In 2021, I made the life-changing decision to get myself unstuck, but as I embarked on a two-year deep-dive healing journey, I realized I had no idea how challenging the transition would be. When we want change, we must accept the challenges that come with it. I spent many days crying, processing years of unacknowledged emotion and releasing deep-seated trauma that had been stored in my body. It was one of the most difficult periods of my life. I grieved and let go of my old life and the old version of me. The pain was real. There were days when things got so tough that I thought my world was going to end. Without my determination to use my experience to inspire others, I probably would have fallen into depression. Throughout this period of patiently allowing myself to go through the deep healing process, I was working as an energy healing practitioner, which at times helped me reveal old wounds of my own.

As I'm reviewing the final draft of this book, my relationship with my then-husband, the father of my child, has reached a much more harmonious place. For me, this shift has come through a daily practice of reflection, emotional healing, and rewiring my thought patterns since our separation. On his part, the intensity of his anger towards my leaving has finally started to dissolve. It is only now that I feel I can truly talk about it from a place of love and understanding, rather than from a place of hurt and sadness.

It is exactly because of this lived experience that I feel so strongly about sharing what I have learned. My intention is not to tell others what to do, but to offer a perspective that might help someone navigate change with more clarity, compassion, and self-awareness. Whether it's a relationship breakdown, the loss of a job, or a personal reckoning, my hope is that readers will find tools here to support them in working through their challenges, shifting old narratives, and moving forward in a way that feels empowering and true to who they are, simply by learning to listen to their own inner wisdom.

I feel strangely giddy when I reflect on how far I have come in my personal growth. So much has changed in my life that I feel like I'm now living a brand-new identity that truly represents who I am—the person I was always meant to be. My intention for my work as a wellness creative and coach is to share my knowledge and learnings with those who may find them useful. My aim is to lead by example, guide with compassion, and heal with love.

To truly get yourself unstuck, you must start with self-awareness. This means observing your thoughts, emotions, and experiences without taking things personally. Self-awareness asks you to notice how you respond, and to ask yourself: Why does this situation trigger me? What old wounds or beliefs am I still holding onto? How can I break free of these patterns so they no longer control me? By watching your inner landscape with curiosity rather than judgement, you gain clarity on what is happening beneath the surface. This is the spark that ignites a transformative process, one that carries you through healing past wounds, reshaping your habits, and stepping fully into the life you are meant to live.

Our preferences—likes or dislikes—are often shaped by past experiences. We tend to hold on to what once made us feel safe, even if it no longer serves us, while avoiding situations or people that caused pain or discomfort. This attachment to familiar patterns, typically rooted in a need for safety, can trap us in cycles that hinder growth. Similarly, avoidant behaviours frequently arise as a defence mechanism to protect ourselves from perceived threats or emotional pain. These behaviours can cause us to distance ourselves not only from others, but also from our feelings, limiting our ability to connect deeply or be vulnerable.

To live a truly fulfilling life, we must break free from ingrained patterns of attachment and avoidance. This means recognizing how past wounds influence our present choices and consciously choosing to step beyond the comfort zone of familiar yet limiting behaviours. It is only by facing our fears, embracing discomfort, and cultivating healthy connections with ourselves and others that we can experience authentic freedom and joy.

Healing plays a significant role in the process of getting unstuck. Without healing, we are unconsciously repeating behavioural patterns based on our limiting beliefs and past experiences, while constantly reacting to life circumstances out of fear. If you truly wish to improve your life, you need to start with a clean slate. This involves returning to the core of your being, unlearning everything you believe to be your identity and reconnecting with your authentic self.

Healing is not about fixing anyone or anything. It does not involve holding people accountable for their actions or fighting for justice. It is certainly not about blaming others for your misfortunes or trying to justify what you have done or what has been done to you. Healing is, in fact, about processing our emotions and learning from our pain or discomfort so that we can respond rather than react to life circumstances. It is a fundamental step in personal growth and transformation. Healing requires us to be brave and vulnerable, embracing both the light and the darkness, and integrating our higher self, our shadow self, and all that exists between the extremes of our contrasting qualities. By healing our unresolved trauma and inner child wounds, we take responsibility for our feelings, preventing ourselves from projecting them onto others and expecting them to fix or complete us. We have all been hurt and traumatized in some way, and it is our responsibility to take ownership of our own healing so that we can present the best versions of ourselves and be of service to others.

A healing journey is the gateway to our core being, our soul, where our true essence is revealed and fully embraced. By understanding that who we are today has been shaped and moulded by past experiences, we can instigate change and reclaim our innate ability to create our destiny. We each possess our own uniqueness, and it takes courage to express ourselves fully without feeling alienated by society and outdated expectations. For years, I judged myself for not living a 'standard life', but what is a standard life? Why should I live as others do? Who set these standards in the first place? I have learned to block out what others deem right or wrong. We all have the right to free will, and it is up to us to make and own our life choices. We may not always be right, but we must bear the consequences of every decision we make. When we choose this path, we live with integrity—there is no one else to blame for our misfortunes or mistakes. We take charge of our own destiny and learn to move with the ebb and flow of life.

The Origin of UNSTUCK

October 2022, 3 a.m.—a dark night for the soul

I was lying in my bed, with pain throbbing in my chest and my throat getting tighter and tighter, thinking, 'Why is this happening to me?' As I closed my eyes and indulged in more heartfelt tears, a divine message came to me—an inner knowing that rose from deep within: 'One day, you will have the strength to turn all this pain into power, and when that day comes, you will share your story with the world.'

As I lay in bed, I reflected on how I had arrived at this moment. Then an inner voice gently urged me: 'Step out of your headspace, connect with your heart, and start writing.' I had always dreamed of writing a book, but now I finally felt ready, not just to tell my story, but to share my experience and an important message with the world: how to get unstuck and find freedom.

When my marriage came to an end, I was met with months of heavy emotions, from anger and resentment to disappointment and sadness. I had decided to leave the marriage when I reached boiling point, which meant I hadn't given myself enough time to fully understand the consequences of ending a fifteen-year co-dependent relationship until the grieving process began.

The grieving process following a loss is incredibly challenging and requires time, love, and patience, as well as a significant amount of solitude, to get to the end of the tunnel where 'rebirth' can take place. The natural response to a separation or any ending is often to start something new or find a replacement. It didn't take me long to enter another connection, only to realize I was repeating the same patterns, but this time they were magnified and played out even more clearly. That was when I knew I needed to pause and do a proper reset to get out of a self-defeating cycle. So, for the first time in decades, I chose to stand on my own and embarked on a journey of self-discovery that required me to relearn everything about my life and myself. Was I scared? Yes. Did I feel lonely? Absolutely. Was it worth it? A million times yes. If I hadn't given myself the time and space to fully reflect on my life and connect the dots to see how I got to where I was, I would have continued the same narrative and achieved the same result over and over again.

I began the process of self-enquiry by questioning all my past relationships and all the behavioural patterns I had repeated. I soon realized that my belief system was driving these patterns, particularly the need to belong and be accepted. My people-pleasing tendencies began to emerge, revealing a hidden and desperate need to please and impress that surfaced in every aspect of my life. Many of us are raised to believe that love means self-sacrifice, meaning we would do anything for the sake of love. Sounds romantic, right? This concept is precisely why so many of us choose to sacrifice for love; it has been romanticized and ingrained in us by media, feeding our egos and glorifying the roles of the fixer, hero, and saviour. It makes us feel 'good' to give ourselves up for others. At its core, this all boils down to one thing: fear.

Our fear of not being good enough often drives us to seek validation and approval from others, which becomes the benchmark for determining our worth. Playing the role of a martyr can make us feel important, good enough, and deserving of love and appreciation. While this illusion provides momentary satisfaction, over time, suppressing emotions such as resentment and anger through constant self-sacrifice can distort our perspectives and lead to self-sabotaging behaviours. When we take on the fixer role, we enable others' behaviours by assuming accountability for their actions, denying their ability to progress. We may believe we are helping them, but in reality, we are allowing their behaviours to continue and trapping them and ourselves in a toxic relationship dynamic.

Someone with a fixer mentality tends to attract or be drawn to individuals who exhibit some form of toxic behaviour or addiction—people who appear to need rescuing. The idea of having a 'project' really makes a fixer tick. In this dynamic, the person being 'saved' places the fixer on a pedestal, which solidifies the fixer's status and the responsibilities tied to it. These responsibilities feed the ego of the fixer, while the other person deflects responsibility and consequences. If left unaddressed, fixers tend to repeat the cycle of finding someone to fix, just as those seeking rescue continue searching for someone to save them. Both parties will continue to attract the same types of relationships to fulfil their respective roles, unless this behaviour is recognized and addressed through healing. The initial phase of such a relationship is always intensely romantic, but it eventually leads to an overly co-dependent and deeply entangled dynamic. Unless we examine the root cause of such a mindset, we will simply repeat the same narrative with whomever comes into our lives.

When we recognize these repeated patterns we begin to understand that unless we choose to break them, it will be impossible to get unstuck. Letting go of the fixer role has allowed me to fully grasp my lack of self-worth. By acknowledging this and addressing the root cause of my past limiting behaviours, I finally broke through the surface, gasping for air after struggling in the depths of the ocean for most of my life.

Self-awareness is the main tool we use for getting unstuck, and I will mention it throughout this book. The other key ingredients are self-love and acceptance. This may sound straightforward, but once we start analysing the meaning of self-love, we realize how easy it is to experience self-neglect instead. Self-neglect means depriving ourselves of our essential needs and desires. Fixers and people-pleasers suffer from self-neglect, as they look for external validation for everything they do or say. This is a sign of not feeling whole, usually because our needs were not met in childhood, and in order to feel safe and worthy of love, respect, and attention, we tend to do whatever it takes to let others determine our worth and provide a sense of security. In short, we give our power away, and when we feel powerless, we continue to seek validation from others to fill that void and alleviate the feeling of incompleteness and, ultimately, the sense of loneliness.

The key to inner joy is to completely love and accept who we are. When we have healthier relationships with ourselves, our thoughts and feelings begin to shift, and our experiences naturally change as a result. We realize that we have the ability to attract what we want in our lives just by focusing on our inner being. This is when transformation begins.

* * *

Not many people knew I had hit rock bottom in 2022. On the surface, I was still showing up and doing the work I was meant to do. However, behind the scenes, my desire to get unstuck drove me to research extensively. I immersed myself in hundreds of books on healing, personal growth, and self-development. What began as a personal healing journey soon inspired me to share my insights with family, friends, and clients. Tools like Emotional Freedom Technique (EFT), cognitive reframing, and energy balancing, which I will elaborate on in this book, became lifelines that helped me navigate some of my darkest moments. What became clear to me along the way was that healing isn't only about what happens in solitude because life doesn't stop for our healing. We still have to live.

Fundamentally, it comes down to how you choose to show up each day. Even after a night of soul-searching or crying so hard you find it hard to breathe, or after experiencing those raw moments in therapy when everything feels like it's falling apart, you still get to decide how you begin again the next morning. If there is one piece of advice I can give you before you begin your journey to get unstuck, it is to see it as a process. In other words, it's a new, different way of living. Nothing in your life has to stop. You can still live as you always have. Subtle changes come over time, and getting unstuck doesn't require you to make huge, dramatic changes. All it requires is your commitment to the process.

One thing I have learned is that being on a healing journey doesn't mean you have to walk around feeling sad, heavy, or having to shut down. You can still show up with a smile, bring light to others, and keep going without pretending everything's perfect. It's not about faking it; it's about understanding that your healing work is only part of your life, and it doesn't have to be your whole identity.

A big shift happened for me when I started practising what Buddhists call 'being the witness'. It means learning to observe what you are feeling without getting completely swept up in it. When you become the witness, even the hardest moments start to feel more like experiences you are having, rather than who you are. It's like watching a movie, you can sit back and notice what is playing out without being pulled into the chaos of the scene. And some days, showing up means not showing up, and that's okay too. Knowing when to retreat, when to rest, when to be soft and vulnerable is equally important. I call it the hermit mode. It's a conscious pause that allows healing to integrate.

Today, as a wellness creative and coach, I have compiled all that I know into a simple framework to serve as a guideline for living a purposeful life, one that we truly desire and are meant to lead. My aim is to share the knowledge and wisdom I have acquired to assist those who feel stuck but are unsure of where or how to begin. Without my spiritual beliefs, I would not have been able to maintain a positive outlook during the process of becoming unstuck.

With that perspective, I consider myself a lifelong seeker, always open to learning from everyone I encounter—my peers, and those in my life who display qualities I admire. I'm dedicated to researching, reflecting, and doing the inner work, while also benefitting from the valuable guidance of my mentor of nearly fifteen years. This journey of growth and evolution is something I believe we are all meant to embrace throughout our lives.

So, let the journey of how you can get unstuck begin.

The Beginning of My Healing Journey

Before I began my healing journey, I was going through life without fully realizing how I had been compromising my own needs. Of all the reasons for feeling stuck in my life, the biggest was the loss of my identity. As painful as it was, in 2015 I gave up my interior design business for the sake of my then-husband's job transfer to Singapore and became a trailing spouse. Restarting my interior design business in a new country was challenging, especially with a one-year-old in tow. It wasn't the best year for me, but not many people knew about this as I chose to internalize my disappointment and suffer silently. I chose to 'suck it up'. I very proudly took on the role of being the ultimate fixer. 'As long as my family is happy, then I'm happy,' I said with pride. In my limited mindset, I chose to believe that my happiness came from making sure that everyone else was happy. The chosen path of self-sacrifice gave me a false sense of purpose, which eventually became an escape from the real issues at hand. In short, I became a stay-at-home mum overnight and my career was put on hold. It soon became clear to me that being a good mother and a good wife was no longer enough of a reason to continue living a life that didn't feel fulfilling. I became numb and disconnected.

As I continued putting my own needs aside, I felt increasingly helpless about a recurring issue in my marriage, something that had been present since I'd first met him in 2006 but had worsened after we'd moved to Singapore as the added pressures of family life and new challenges took their toll. The ongoing struggles, including his coping habits, created a deep anxiety in me. No matter how hard I tried to communicate and work things through with him, the weight of it left me exhausted and unsure of how much longer I could hold on. I reached a point where I knew I had to choose either to ignore my mental well-being and tolerate behaviours that were causing me stress and anxiety, or to end a cycle that had become too toxic for me to handle. For many years of our marriage, self-care was a band-aid over unhealed wounds. It was a temporary solution and required regular maintenance, but it also created a blockage in my life force, and I regularly found myself feeling depleted and stuck.

By the time you reach midlife, you'll learn the lessons you need to, whether you're ready or not. It's not always easy or comfortable. Sometimes, you just have to face the tough stuff head-on, question what you have been telling yourself, and be real about what's holding you back. That is where the real healing starts, when you strip away all the old stories and get back to your true self. Lasting change requires a huge amount of soul-searching and reprogramming of the body and mind.

I received my first wake-up call in 2016 when I was admitted to the hospital due to an alarmingly low white blood cell count. The doctors told me that my body wasn't producing enough white blood cells to protect me from infection, and I would need to be monitored closely. They ran numerous tests, but worryingly no one could determine the exact cause. One possibility they mentioned was a condition called Leucopenia, or worst case leukaemia, though nothing was confirmed at that stage. Later on, through my own research, I found that Leucopenia can sometimes be linked to autoimmune issues or triggered by prolonged stress, something that made a lot of sense given what I was going through at the time. The uncertainty was difficult to sit with, especially since the information was delivered in a surprisingly casual way. I broke down in the hospital ward that evening, trying to process it all on my own. It was a wake-up call, all right. One I didn't see coming.

I started reflecting on my life, on what I had and hadn't done, on the things that did and didn't matter to me. The only person I was worried about was my daughter, and the consequences of my potential absence from her life if the diagnosis proved to be something serious. The fear I endured that day was indescribable. I couldn't fathom the reality of being away from my two-year-old. I questioned whether I had the strength to face the potential challenges that lay ahead of me. As I lay in the hospital bed, feeling extremely lost and mentally deflated, I decided to speak to the universe directly for the first time in my life:

> God, the Higher Power, the Universe, please help me conquer this so I can be reunited with my daughter. I promise you I will not take this for granted and I will live my life to the fullest from this point onwards. I promise I will continue to learn the meaning of life and will spread the message so others can benefit from it. Please bring me home to my daughter safely.

And then, there was my answer: three birds flew past as I looked out of the window. Somehow, intuitively, I knew deep within me that this was the response I had desperately needed—I'd got a yes.

Miraculously, my white blood cell count started to increase the following morning, and within two days, I was discharged and ready to return home to my family. Having surrendered to the Universe, I kept my promise, and I immersed myself in various healing modalities for the next six years. This marked the beginning of my training as an energy healing practitioner, which formed the foundation of my wellness business. I chose to use the opportunity to live life fully again. I started to live life as I knew I was supposed to—to heal, balance, and liberate.

Part I

The Feeling of 'Stuckness'

'If you were born with the weakness to fall you were born with the strength to rise.'

—Rupi Kaur

1

Why Do We Feel Stuck?

Have you ever wondered what people daydream about when they're commuting to work on the train, waiting in a queue for coffee, or taking a stroll in the park? Most people fantasize about things they don't have: a different scenario, a different career path, a different partner, a different life. The more we fantasize about an alternative path, the more disconnected we feel from our current one. When you wake up from that perfect daydream, reality kicks in, and often, you feel even worse than you had before your mind wandered off to fantasy land. You feel stuck in a reality that does not align with who you are deep down, and worst of all, there is a constant need to put on a façade and keep playing your expected role in society.

We humans are masters of distraction. We escape from things we don't want to face in order to create a false sense of comfort. Excessive behaviours such as shopping, gambling, phone scrolling, drinking, and partying offer a temporary rescue from a meaningless way of living. Brené Brown, a renowned researcher on vulnerability and courage, explains that the strategies we use to numb our vulnerability don't just numb the darkness, they also numb the light. When we actively avoid negative emotions, we also suppress the good ones: love, joy, and belonging.[1]

---

[1] Brené Brown, *Daring Greatly: How the Courage to Be Vulnerable Transforms the Way We Live, Love, Parent, and Lead* (Penguin Publishing Group, 2012), chapter 4, eBook.

For most of us, there is a clarity about what we don't want. But how do we know what we truly desire and how do we take steps towards our dream lives?

According to Dr Bruce H. Lipton—whose internationally recognized work bridges science and spirituality—by the time we reach adulthood, we are running a set of behavioural 'programmes' on autopilot. These habits and patterns, repeated unconsciously every day, form a fixed framework that gives us the illusion of security and comfort.[2] However, this illusion becomes a trap, limiting our potential. The decisions we make are often based on our childhood conditioning, with each thought and emotion reinforcing our existing beliefs. Over time, these beliefs shape our personality—how we perceive the world and how we express ourselves within it.

You might be wondering: What's wrong with running these programmes? In truth, there's nothing wrong with being on autopilot. It's how we cycle, drive, or swim. That's the beauty of learning—we practise until the subconscious mind can take over. The conscious (logical) mind learns and absorbs, and once new skills are imprinted into the subconscious, they can be performed without active thought. But if we remain on autopilot 24/7, no changes will ever be made. When we keep recycling the same thoughts and emotions, and repeating the same behaviours, there's no room for growth. More and more people are waking up to this realization. This is the reason why self-improvement and the art of manifestation have gained so much attention; we are finally slowly waking up from what I call the zombie state.

Zombie state is life lived on autopilot. It's where excitement, curiosity, hope, and joy are missing as we relentlessly repeat the past, just in different formats. Each time we repeat a reaction,

---

[2] Bruce H. Lipton, *The Biology of Belief: Unleashing the Power of Consciousness, Matter and Miracles*, (ReadHowYouWant, 2010), chapter 7.

we reaffirm it in our subconscious mind, making it harder and harder to change the way we think and feel. This toxic cycle traps us in survival mode, one that is filled with stress and anxiety, which slowly eats away at the joy and peace in our lives.

Who wants to live like this? Not me.

When we are in a zombie state, we move through life unconsciously, disconnected from our thoughts, feelings, and behaviours. We feel numb but have a deep knowing that something is missing. Life simply feels uninspired and without a clear purpose. One of the symptoms of such a state is chronic venting and complaining. We go on about how unhappy we are, yet take no action to change it. We find ourselves repeatedly vocalizing dissatisfaction that puts us in a low vibrational state[3] and only serves to further reinforce our sense of misery. The more we complain, the more stuck and frustrated we feel, and the more we recreate the same reality. Our minds become numb, and we continue living unaligned and unconscious lives, trapped in a daily cycle of repeated negative thought—emotion loops.

But here's the truth: we have complete control over our thoughts, and our state of mind depends on the quality of those thoughts. When we think stressful thoughts, our minds become agitated, which in turn affects how we feel and what actions we take. What many of us don't realize is that every thought generates an emotion, and that emotion becomes linked to the thought itself. The more we feel the emotion, the more we repeat the thought. Eventually, we become completely weighed down with emotional baggage and distorted perspectives, losing touch with who we are and what matters to us most.

---

[3] In energy work, low vibrations refer to negative experiences, qualities, and emotions that are out of sync with our true selves. A low vibrational state may indicate a person struggling with self-inflicted problems and resistance towards life.

Meanwhile, our attention gets pulled in all directions, scattered across endless distractions, responsibilities, and noise. This mental fragmentation makes it even harder to ground ourselves or gain clarity. Without conscious awareness, we end up reacting rather than responding, slipping into unconscious choices and disconnecting from our authentic selves. We run the same old programmes, day in and day out, until we reach the next holiday we have been counting down to since the last one, when we briefly escaped daily life and forgot how empty it felt. If we don't understand why we feel stuck, we'll have no clue about how to get out of it.

Zombie state sucks because we are stuck in a cycle of past thoughts, emotions, and behaviours, and we can't see a way out of it. Every time we react to a 'threat', we strengthen the very coping mechanism that caused the stuckness to begin with. Making decisions from this place only reinforces limiting beliefs—that life is unfair, and the world is unsafe.

Living in a zombie state means living in constant fear. The stress response controls our daily experience. Life becomes inauthentic, and we begin living by conditions of worth—criteria set by others. We strive to gain approval by meeting external expectations, but the pain begins when those expectations don't align with our soul. That subtle but persistent whisper saying, 'Something doesn't feel right,' is the first sign of inner misalignment. Even though we all have the ability to sense it, only a small percentage of people are brave enough to act on it.

When our lives are dictated by what we've experienced in the past, we end up living in defence mode, operating from a place of avoiding past hurt and pain. We navigate life from a fearful place, one that is focused on threat and danger, rather than from a place of love and safety. When we live as though threat and danger are just around the corner, we activate the body's fight-or-flight response. This is an automatic survival mechanism triggered by acute stress where the sympathetic nervous system releases a cascade of hormones. As a result, the heart rate spikes, blood pressure rises, and breathing becomes rapid and shallow.

Although this response is vital in life-threatening situations, it's only meant to be temporary. The body should return to a balanced state once the perceived threat is gone. Furthermore, this state of heightened stress becomes chronic as they remain in survival mode long after the initial stressor has passed. This disrupts the body's homeostatic balance and can lead to a range of physical and mental health issues. The long-term effects of living in fight-or-flight mode are not only damaging, they can also be irreversible. We will explore the nervous system in more detail in Part II.

2

Why Do We Remain Stuck?

We are creatures of habit. Even when we feel unhappy or dissatisfied, the routines we operate on autopilot are so deeply ingrained that they create an illusion of security. These habitual patterns—emotional, behavioural, and cognitive form a familiar territory. As a result, even though we recognize the need for change, we often find ourselves trapped in a continuous loop, repeating self-defeating thoughts and experiencing negative emotions.

In this state, we are no longer in creative mode, where possibility can occur. Instead, we're simply surviving, replaying the same emotions, engaging in the same habits, the same limiting patterns, all while suffering silently and hoping the pain will somehow disappear. But transformation doesn't happen by chance. It begins the moment we acknowledge that real change starts from within. Only then can the outer world begin to respond to the inner shifts. Breaking out of this stuckness requires more than insight; it takes inner work, strength, resilience, and a willingness to challenge what's familiar. Even though it might be difficult work, it is work that is possible for anyone who truly believes they're ready for change to do.

When we consciously choose to break free from old patterns and release the weight of past experiences, we tap into Zen Buddhism's concept of a beginner's mind: a mindset of openness, curiosity, and freedom from expectation. It's the same way children engage with the world, eager to explore, express, and discover, unburdened by judgement. Children embody this natural sense of wonder and express themselves freely, until at some point, authority figures begin introducing rules and expectations. As a parent myself, I know how difficult it can be to strike the right balance between nurturing free will and providing structure. Of course, some form of guidance is necessary in parenting, but through my own healing, coaching clients, and reflecting on my upbringing, I've come to see that many of us lose our sense of joy and wonder somewhere along the way.

We learn to conform to be accepted and approved. Many of us were taught, implicitly or explicitly, that love is conditional, that it's when we are well-behaved and seen as 'good' that we are rewarded. This becomes our model for love. We learn to perform, to please, to meet standards, often losing touch with our authentic selves in the process. Later in life, this turns into a quest for validation, a need to prove our worth to others and to ourselves.

This pattern is so deeply embedded in our society that few ever question it. Those who rebel are often labelled misfits or outcasts, while those who conform are praised, given status, and held up as examples. We become burdened with expectations, overly critical of others and especially of ourselves. Joy, spontaneity, and presence become elusive because we're filtering life through the lens of our past conditioning.

The first step towards liberation is to reclaim our childlike wonder and embrace a beginner's mind. It means suspending our expectations, judgements, assumptions, and preferences, and allowing life to surprise us. How magnificent would it be to move through the world with such openness and curiosity?

During the process of getting myself unstuck, there were times when I doubted the decisions I had made and the steps I had taken to break free from the patterns, fears, and beliefs that had kept me stuck for so long. Self-doubt is an old friend of mine that likes to visit from time to time, but with self-awareness, any default settings can be adjusted and modified. When you realize that your limiting beliefs are stopping you from progressing any further, remember to pause and reflect on the emotions you are feeling. It is important to always check in with your emotions and shift your perspective accordingly to snap out of the negative loop of self-sabotage. Listing things that no longer serve you and finding out what you truly want will help you to remain focused on the end goal—to become unstuck.

Life is made up of a series of choices. Stagnation is unsustainable in the long run, and you don't want to wait until life gets too 'sticky' to shift your reality. If something is not working out for you, you have two options: find a way to make it work or find your way out. Staying where you are and doing nothing means you will be stuck in that situation forever.

The main culprits to look out for when you find it hard to get unstuck are:

- Fear
- Discomfort
- Indecision
- Allowing others to dictate our future
- Not trusting or listening to our intuition
- Inner resistance

Fear

At the heart of it, fear is often what keeps people stuck in situations that bring them no joy. It's hard to imagine any other reason someone would choose to live a joyless life.

Let's look at the reasons behind this fear. Fear of the unknown is the type of fear that I see most often in my clients because, as humans, we want everything to be predictable. Renowned mental health expert and speaker Gabor Maté explains this in his book *When the Body Says No: The Cost of Hidden Stress*, that psychological factors such as uncertainty and lack of control are the most common triggers for activating our stress response.[4] Anything known represents safety and security. We know roughly what the outcome will be, which minimizes the risk of unwanted surprises or uncertainty. We simply do not like to be kept in the dark, not knowing what is going on in the present or what will happen in the future. The more 'unsafe' we feel in the world we live in, the more 'control' we think we need to feel safe.

This way of thinking not only creates a lot of stress (since life is full of surprises whether you like it or not), it also prevents us from living in creative mode and in alignment with what our hearts truly desire. If you tune into the energy of the word 'control', how does it make you feel? For me, there's a lot of resistance. The energy creates a blockage in the system and makes me feel fearful. The need to be in control is a coping strategy that puts us in survival mode, which does not allow us to tap into our creative capacity as our minds are too busy working out how to cope and survive.

When we're afraid of the unknown, we tend to stay in our comfort zones. Our repetitive daily routines feel predictable, and we're good at running those automated programmes. It's easy because it doesn't take much effort and offers a sense of certainty, something we all crave. These repeated narratives help us feel safe, even though they're also keeping us stuck and unfulfilled.

The need to feel safe holds us in a comfort bubble, one that limits our opportunities and stunts our growth. Comfort is often what keeps us stuck in situations that no longer serve us. It keeps us small and holds us back from reaching our full potential. Ultimately, it exists because of fear.

Our brains are wired to keep us safe and activate our survival instincts when needed. The brain is constantly scanning for

---

4 Gabor Maté, *When the Body Says No: The Cost of Hidden Stress* (Wiley, 2011), chapter 7, eBook.

danger so that we can prepare our fight-or-flight responses. It's a survival mechanism that goes way back. Our ancestors needed to stay hyper-aware of threats, like predators or danger in the environment to just to stay alive. That same wiring still lives in us today. So even though we're not running from lions any more, our brain still constantly scans for what could go wrong. It holds onto negative experiences more strongly than positive ones, and it reacts faster to fear or criticism than to calm or praise. This means we're naturally more inclined to focus on what's missing, what's not working, or what might go wrong. We might not even realize we're doing this. That's why it's so easy to spiral into worry, self-pity, or worst-case thinking, especially during stressful times.

The truth is that our brain is simply doing its job to protect us. But sometimes, this very protection ends up keeping us stuck instead. The only way to get out of this survival mode is to shift our relationship with fear so that we can liberate ourselves from the fear-based beliefs that we would have accumulated over the course of our lives. When we break free from our past trauma and unhealed wounds, we can move forward with confidence and courage. Fear is a breeding ground for stuckness, as it stifles our thinking and actions. Fear keeps us feeling small and powerless, which keeps us locked in a place that limits our potential.

Here are some common forms of fear:

- Fear of the unknown
- Fear of being judged
- Fear of not being good enough
- Fear of abandonment
- Fear of rejection
- Fear of change
- Fear of success (what it might change)
- Fear of failure

All fearful thoughts, however stubborn, can be corrected by shifting our mindsets and perception. This requires us to work through our fears and dissect each fearful thought and feeling so we can get to its root cause.

Awareness of our thoughts and emotions is a vital part of setting ourselves free, especially when we live in a fear-based society where order is often maintained by instilling fear into daily life. People in positions of authority frequently use fear as a tool to achieve compliance, and it's common for parents to adopt this strategy to gain desired behaviour from their children. Many parents feel the need to maintain control, not only over their own lives but also over how their children turn out. This creates a cycle of fear-driven stress that feels never-ending.

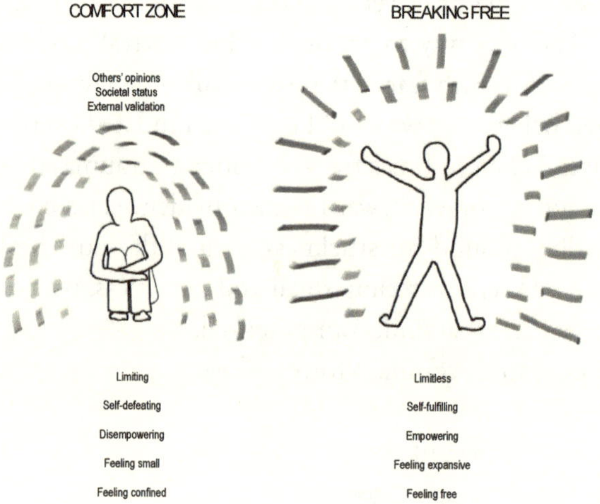

Figure 2.1: Which one resonates with you?[5]

Stephen M. R. Covey, a leadership expert and author, describes the 'Command and Control' framework as

[5] Illustrations by Mae Kwan.

> being efficient with people, trying to motivate them instead of inspiring them. It's about self-interest and competing rather than serving and caring. And if all else fails, it's about barking out the orders so everyone does exactly what they're supposed to do—not because they want to, but because they have to.[6]

Given that this approach is deeply embedded in many areas of society, it's no surprise that most of us find it difficult to break free from fear-based living!

To truly understand how fear sabotages our lives, we must be willing to acknowledge and accept its presence. Fear keeps us in our comfort zone, as the body and mind become conditioned to the constant release of stress hormones and a state of high alert. The stress-related symptoms are often treated with medication, while the underlying cause, chronic stress, remains unaddressed. Because fear activates the body's stress response, learning to regularly tune into our bodies and scanning for tension or discomfort can help us make small adjustments that reduce stress and move us closer to a more balanced state.

Discomfort

Rumi, the Sufi mystic and Iranian poet, said, 'The cure for the pain is in the pain.'[7] The process of healing comprises a series of uncomfortable and sometimes painful moments. This is perhaps why so many of us choose to ignore our unresolved trauma and dismiss our feelings. To get unstuck, we must find courage and develop resilience to carry us through the process. We have to sit

---

6 Stephen M. R. Covey, *Trust & Inspire: How Truly Great Leaders Unleash Greatness in Others* (Simon and Schuster, 2022), 3.

7 Jalal ad-Din Muhammad Rumi, *The Essential Rumi* (HarperCollins Publishers, 1995), trans. Coleman Barks, 205.

with the discomfort to create a channel for the intense emotions to be felt, processed, and metabolized. When this happens, a memory becomes merely an event that happened in the past and no longer has a hold on us. Cultivating the ability to sit with discomfort can help us release the emotions that keep prompting the thinking mind to replay upsetting past events. To break the vicious thought–emotion cycle, we must embrace discomfort, which is the key to emotional freedom. Many experts in the healthcare and wellness industry can safely guide you through the healing process for severe cases of trauma. Finding the right trauma-informed professional will help you take the necessary steps to heal safely.

Indecision

We frequently experience heightened stuckness when we are at a crossroads and struggle to make a decision and move forward. This type of stagnation can last for many years for some people. It might be feeling stuck in an unhappy relationship, not seeing progress in a job, or not reaching an ideal weight no matter how much you exercise. It might be the constant worry about bills, rent, or lingering debt. The list goes on. During times of confusion, our overwhelming thoughts and emotions can make it difficult to look at the situation with a clear mind and find our way forward.

Let's look at why we struggle to make prompt decisions and take action. We often procrastinate when we feel overwhelmed by our thoughts and emotions. Opinions from friends and family add fuel to the fire, which makes it even harder to know which way to turn. What if I make the wrong decision? What if it doesn't work out? This kind of negative self-talk plays on repeat in our minds until we reach a state of complete standstill out of fear. We are not even surviving any more; we are simply frozen.

So much time is wasted when we play out all the possible scenarios in our head in the hope of assessing the risks for each option to minimize the damage or maximize the gain. This thought process is the perfect example of how we love to be in control of everything. As much as we would like to know how things will unfold in the future, life consists of so many unpredictable variables that there is almost no point in overanalysing our options without taking any form of action.

When we start tuning into our inner compass, all the answers are available to us. All we have to do is listen in by staying present. So, how do we listen to this inner guidance? We listen by being still, a state that can only be achieved when our awareness is in the present. Staying present means we do not allow our past experiences to affect how we make our decisions today; we do not waste our energy by projecting into the future. I will explain how we can achieve this later in the book. For now, I want to focus on the reasons for feeling stuck so that you can accept your situation and give yourself permission to be free.

Allowing Others to Dictate Our Future

'What are people going to think?' How many times have you asked yourself this question when making a life-changing decision? If you're asking it, it's probably because you want to do something different, something outside the box.

Humans are social beings, and we have an innate desire to belong. This herd mentality often leads us to feel ashamed of doing anything that the group may not accept, whether it's within our family, community, or society at large. As a result, we may make decisions based on what is expected of us, rather than what feels true. We tend to follow the safe paths that others have taken before us. In doing so, we risk losing our uniqueness and the X factor that sets us apart.

We care too much about what others think, often more than we care about ourselves or the way we live. One of the biggest steps we can take towards self-mastery is to reclaim our power by tuning out the noise and listening to our inner voice. To do this, we must stop engaging with thoughts that hinder our growth and stop giving weight to how others may judge us.

Reclaiming our power creates more mental space for what truly matters. The more we channel our energy into bettering ourselves, the more motivated and energized we feel. Standing in our personal power means living in alignment with our values and prioritizing what's important to us. This is what allows us to live and speak our truth.

Not Trusting or Listening to Our Intuition

All humans possess the precious gift of intuition, but many of us choose to ignore it. Instead, we listen to the opinions of others, which often conflict with our instincts. You must make full use of this special power in the get-unstuck process. When you step out of your comfort zone, there are times when no precedent exists; this is when your intuition becomes your greatest ally. Everyone makes decisions based on their own personal experiences, unresolved issues, and unhealed wounds. Although advice from others can be helpful, ultimately, only you can decide what is best for you. So, how can you do this confidently? By tuning into your intuition and listening to your inner voice, which I will explain later in the book.

In my experience, some people are naturally in touch with their intuition. Although they may not intentionally tune into it regularly, their decisions mostly follow their sense of inner knowing combined with a strong sense of certainty. This certainty reinforces their trust in their intuition and helps them make choices that are aligned with their goals and purpose. These natural-born initiators have the ability to inspire and motivate others.

Inner Resistance

One of the biggest blockers to change is inner resistance, and one of its most common manifestations is our need for control. We often pour our time and energy into trying to control everything around us: people, outcomes, the future. When we operate this way, we're not only exhausting ourselves, we're also creating burnout and mental stagnation. This kind of overload is often mistaken for productivity but in reality, it's resistance in disguise.

At its most extreme, this behaviour can show up as obsessive tendencies like helicopter parenting, micromanaging at work, or overplanning every possible scenario in life. We become consumed by the illusion that if we control every variable, we can avoid failure, disappointment, or discomfort. But what's really going on underneath? At the root of this obsessive need to control is fear—fear of uncertainty, fear of not being good enough, fear of something going wrong. It ultimately stems from a deep sense of feeling unsafe. This need for control is often shaped by earlier life experiences. If we weren't given consistent emotional support or were raised in unpredictable environments, our nervous systems may have developed a default setting of hypervigilance. As adults, we replicate those patterns by overcompensating, trying to stay one step ahead of everything and everyone. We resist change, not because we're lazy or unmotivated, but because change threatens the illusion of safety we've worked so hard to maintain.

But here's the truth: control does not equal safety. In fact, our obsessive attempts to control the uncontrollable often make us feel more anxious, not less. Real safety comes from within, by developing emotional resilience, trusting ourselves, and building a grounded relationship with the present moment.

It's essential to recognize the difference between what we can and can't control, so we can redirect our energy wisely.

We can control:

- Our thoughts (with practice and awareness)
- Our emotions (reflect underlying issues and signal what needs attention)
- Our inner dialogue (self-talk)
- Our boundaries (what we allow or don't allow)
- What we give our energy to or focus on
- Who we surround ourselves with
- How we respond to challenges
- Our perception and mindset

We can't control:

- Past events
- Future events
- Other people's opinions, beliefs, or expectations
- How others think, feel, or behave
- What others say about us
- How people react to our boundaries
- Being liked or accepted by everyone
- Unexpected events

When we stop fighting reality and start working with it, resistance begins to soften. This shift allows energy to flow more freely, giving us greater clarity, emotional strength, and the ability to respond rather than react. Getting unstuck doesn't always require drastic action. It often begins with a quiet decision to let go of what we can't control and to focus on creating safety and strength within.

Inner resistance is not something to eliminate overnight. It's something to understand, acknowledge, and work with. The more we learn to recognize the fear underneath our need for control, the more empowered we become to move through it on our terms, in our own time.

3

How to Get Unstuck: Breaking Free from Fear-Based Thought Patterns

One thing we have complete control over is our minds. With self-awareness, we can master our minds by preventing ourselves from dwelling on negative thoughts. We can change how we feel by freeing ourselves from the emotional burden of fear-based thought patterns and returning to a neutral state.

When fear lingers, it's a sign that a limiting belief is slowly creeping back to sabotage the progress you've made. If that happens, take a step back, readjust your mindset, and focus on making small changes instead. It takes time to reverse beliefs you've carried for many years, so be gentle with yourself, take a deep breath, and carry on.

To shift away from fear-based thinking, we need to change the way we speak to ourselves and become aware of our inner critics. Replace thoughts like, 'I'm scared of the unknown. What's going to happen to me? I might lose everything,' with, 'The unknown is an open field full of possibilities. It is a new beginning, and everything is going to happen for me from this point onwards. I trust.'

Replace, 'What are people going to think? What if they believe I've made a terrible mistake by leaving my job? What if they're right and I end up jobless for years to come?' with, 'I know what I want, and I'm confident that the decisions I make will turn out to be the best ones for me. I believe in myself.'

Replace, 'I'm scared of failing. What if everything goes horribly wrong? I don't have the ability to get through this,' with, 'Stepping into the unknown gives me the opportunity to create positive change and better outcomes. I trust that I have the ability to make it happen. I believe.'

There are times when positive thinking can feel forced, because a part of us doesn't truly believe the affirmations we're repeating. For instance, when we say, 'I believe in myself', we might actually be thinking, 'I don't really believe in myself, so I need to say this over and over to hide my insecurity.'

An affirmation only serves its purpose when we genuinely believe what we're saying to be true. If there's a disconnect, it's often because of limiting beliefs buried in the subconscious that need to be acknowledged and rewired. For affirmations to be effective, our words must align with how we feel deep inside. This alignment can only be achieved through inner work, by reflecting on what's holding us back, exploring the root of the belief or emotion, and rewriting the narrative to create lasting change.

Life is made up of the decisions we make every day. When those decisions are mostly driven by fear, they can lead to poor judgement and unaligned choices, since fear is the fuel that keeps us operating in survival mode. The need to protect ourselves often stems from unmet emotional needs in childhood. When the essential foundations for healthy development aren't fully provided, a child may develop coping mechanisms to stay safe and avoid getting hurt. To free ourselves from the past, we must address the pain and trauma we experienced in childhood. Beginning to investigate why we feel unsafe can give us the perspective and agency to move through life in a more positive and empowered way.

Holding on to fear-based beliefs limits our ability to thrive. Fear locks us into a scarcity mindset, where we obsess over what's missing. This never-ending, self-destructive cycle reinforces the belief that we're not enough, don't have enough, and aren't doing enough, and that there isn't enough to go around. As we begin to shift our beliefs and lean into a growth mindset, we open ourselves to the possibility of turning things around.

Resilience is a buzzword in personal growth because while no one goes through life without facing challenges, the mindset we choose to adopt when faced with them can make a real difference. A scarcity mindset creates feelings of lack, insecurity, and competition regardless of how successful we are. These underlying feelings feed into stressful thoughts and self-sabotaging behaviours, keeping us stuck in unhelpful patterns.

Change can only take place when we change our perspectives during difficult times, and our perspectives are formed by our beliefs and past experiences. We can choose how we react to external circumstances or rather, to respond by looking at every situation with a clear lens. This involves understanding the meaning behind the situation and determining the best way to respond. To get unstuck, our focus should be on changing our beliefs so we can dream, create, and move towards the life we truly want. In this way, we can tap into the abundance mindset where all things are possible. When we operate from an abundance mindset, we no longer focus on what we lack but on the possibilities of achieving and receiving. This change in perspective enables us to direct our attention towards finding solutions and moving forward.

In my work helping clients restore mental, emotional, and physical balance, I've noticed a common theme underlying their stuckness: unnoticed misalignment. They come feeling stressed, overwhelmed, exhausted, unable to sleep, and trapped in stagnation. Their energy is low, they feel blocked and stuck, and their sense of balance slips away. But somehow, there's a quiet acceptance fuelled by the assumption that this is how everyone lives—in a place of suffering. Many seek singing bowl meditation or therapy sessions for relief, but I've found that stress management alone is often just a band-aid. It doesn't produce lasting change. Trauma and stuck emotions become trapped in the body, and while healing modalities can help release stored tension and emotional pain, unless the root cause is addressed, triggers continue to arise and emotional pain festers.

Breaking free requires more than detoxing negative emotions; it demands a change in the thought patterns that fuel the thought–emotion cycle. A common misconception is that stress is caused by external circumstances, when our response to those circumstances determines our stress level. Our stress level reflects our emotional balance. The fewer inner wounds and unresolved triggers we carry, the more peaceful our lives become. Stress is essentially the accumulated effect of suppressed emotions from the past, influencing how we feel and behave in the present. This leads to anxiety and a growing need for control as we try to protect ourselves from getting hurt again.

Limiting beliefs, formed in childhood, distort our perception of reality. For example, if you experienced betrayal from a friend, you might unconsciously adopt the belief that people can't be trusted, which then colours how you approach new relationships. Recognizing and releasing these limiting beliefs clears the lens through which we view the world, allowing us to respond to situations with fresh, neutral perspectives.

Similarly, if you grew up with overly critical or opinionated parents, their judgements don't just shape your worldview; they often become your inner voice—the inner critic that repeats their commentary. This internalized criticism impacts how you live your life and undermines your confidence. Focusing solely on stress management without shifting these perceptions means balance remains elusive. Under heavy stress and survival mode, effective problem-solving becomes nearly impossible.

Many books offer guidance on healing, finding balance, and manifesting your dream life, but how do these concepts connect? More importantly, how do we integrate them into daily life? Life is a series of highs and lows, predictable routines punctuated by unexpected twists and turns. As the saying goes, 'Life is like a rollercoaster. You can either scream or enjoy the ride.' Some people adapt to change with ease, but for most of us, instability can feel deeply unsettling, especially when we rely on safety and stability for comfort and reassurance.

When life feels uncertain, our sense of safety is compromised. This can trigger old, limiting beliefs such as not being good enough, capable enough, or worthy of good things. In response, we might procrastinate, self-sabotage, or revert to familiar coping mechanisms. This is the nervous system doing its best to protect us from perceived threats, even if that threat is simply the fear of change.

Understanding this can be the first step towards breaking the cycle. We need to recognize what's happening beneath the surface. By embracing life's cyclical nature, we can empower ourselves to honour our emotions when triggered, recognize and transform patterns, and take actions that align us with our authentic selves. In doing so, we begin to move with the universe's rhythm rather than resisting it.

My UNSTUCK framework offers an overview of this self-development journey, along with practical tools to support you at every stage.

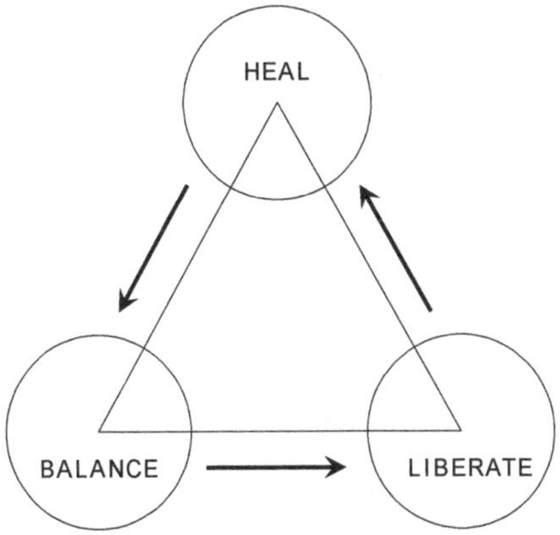

Figure 3.1: Phases in the UNSTUCK framework

There are three phases in the UNSTUCK framework: heal, balance, and liberate. The framework is based on the notion that it is impossible to maintain balance and unleash our creative capacity without doing the necessary healing work to transform the beliefs that are holding us back from our greatness. Healing is a process of identifying preconditioned beliefs from our childhood so that we can come back to our true, authentic selves.

Heal Balance Liberate

Figure 3.2: An artistic rendition of the UNSTUCK framework[8]

When we heal, we:

- Become aware of our emotions
- Process our emotions and let them move through us
- Let go with acceptance and acknowledgement
- Become aware of thoughts and behavioural patterns
- Realign with our authentic selves

---

[8] The author created a series called *Isolation* that includes the illustrations of 'Heal', 'Balance', and 'Liberate' as seen above. This series was created during the pandemic, which was when the UNSTUCK framework concept first emerged. The collection was launched at Design Orchard in 2021. The prints of the collection are still available on the author's website: https://www.maselifestyle.com/shop/crystal-art-prints

When we balance, we:

- Practise staying present
- Tune in and decompress
- Declutter our thoughts and detox our emotions
- Form new habits and build resilience
- Anchor the energy and stay on the path

When we liberate, we:

- Stay in alignment
- Ignite passion
- Find joy
- Practise gratitude
- Create in the flow

The UNSTUCK framework offers reference points we can turn to as we navigate the ever-changing phases of life. It provides not only a structured path but also a set of practical tools to help us build and maintain momentum, especially when we feel overwhelmed, confused, or emotionally blocked.

4

Why the Get-UNSTUCK Journey Is Cyclical

In recent years, many people have become captivated by the idea of consciously creating the life they desire. We see practices like the 369 method, vision boards, and affirmation loops gaining traction across social media and in self-help circles. These tools can be useful for clarifying goals and intentions, but they only scratch the surface.

Based on my research, personal experience, and years of working with clients, I've discovered that true transformation cannot occur through mindset work alone. You can't achieve real change simply by repeating affirmations if the underlying 'hardware', aka your belief system, habits, emotional imprints, and nervous system, remains unchanged.

That's why the UNSTUCK framework is not linear. It's a cyclical process of healing, balancing, and liberating that we move through repeatedly as life unfolds. Each cycle takes us deeper. Each return offers new awareness, growth, and clarity. The work is never done because we are constantly evolving. Life doesn't just throw challenges at us, it mirrors back what's unresolved within us, revealing patterns and wounds that need our attention. Many of the situations and people we encounter hold up a mirror to show us what still needs healing, what lessons to be learned, and where we are being called to grow.

In order to live with clarity, intention, and joy, we need to clear the blocks that keep us repeating old stories. Here's the truth I've come to know:

- You can't create change if your beliefs are still conditioned by your past or shaped by what others expect of you.
- You can't expand when your inner critic is still running the show, replaying fear-based scripts.
- You can't step into your power if your nervous system doesn't feel safe.
- You can't find clarity if your mind is scattered and overwhelmed, stuck in loops of anxiety or worry.
- You can't move forward when your thoughts, emotions, and actions are out of alignment with your truth.
- You can't access flow when your energy is fragmented or constantly leaking outwards.
- You can't respond to life's invitations if you're not present enough to recognize the signs and synchronicities.
- You can't grow if you're still emotionally entangled with the past, carrying unprocessed shame, grief, regret, or resentment.
- You can't create a fulfilling life when you're chasing external validation instead of tuning into your inner voice.
- You can't live authentically if you're afraid to be seen or hiding parts of yourself to stay safe.
- You can't make empowered choices if you're disconnected from your body and intuition.
- You can't thrive if you're constantly numbing your discomfort instead of sitting with it.
- You can't experience true freedom if you're living by someone else's rules or timeline.

- You can't gain momentum if your energy is consumed by people-pleasing or overgiving.
- You can't hear your own guidance if your mind is noisy with comparison or perfectionism.
- You can't act on inner wisdom if you don't trust yourself or life.

The UNSTUCK journey invites you to come home to yourself. It isn't about becoming someone new; it's about peeling back the layers of fear, conditioning, and self-doubt, so you can remember who you've always been underneath it all.

The UNSTUCK framework guides us to heal from unresolved trauma and reprogramme the subconscious beliefs that feed our fears. At its core, it's about cultivating self-love and acceptance, meeting ourselves with compassion, not criticism. When we reconnect with our true, authentic selves, we unlock the ability to express our unique gifts and talents without comparison. Our turning point comes when we truly embrace this truth and begin to live in alignment with it every day.

The journey of self-discovery is deeply personal, and healing is a vital part of that path (heal). But healing alone isn't enough, we also need balance to help us integrate change into our everyday lives in a grounded, sustainable way (balance). Balance is about awareness. It's about learning to stay present, especially when life gets noisy or uncertain. When we cultivate self-awareness and learn to anchor ourselves in the now, we create the space to make conscious choices. And with that clarity and trust in ourselves, we begin to take aligned action towards a more fulfilling, joyful life (liberate).

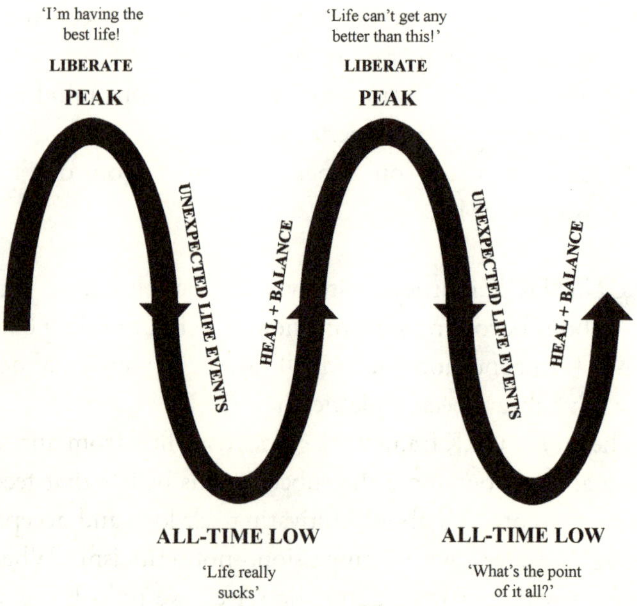

Figure 4.1: Life experience cycle

Key Elements of the UNSTUCK Framework

Vibration

In energy healing work, we work with the concept of vibrational energy. As humans, we're born with a natural ability to sense subtle cues from our environment, but over time, this sensitivity can become suppressed by external influences. Not only can we sense energy, but we also emit it through our thoughts and emotions. Through my work as an energy healing practitioner, I've discovered that energy is indeed contagious. The way someone thinks or feels can directly affect your own state of being, so who you spend time with can have a real impact on your emotional and energetic balance.

During the process of getting unstuck, it is essential to keep a check on our vibrational being, which is directly linked to our thoughts and emotions. Good feelings, such as feeling excited about a dream job or feeling loved by the people around you, raise your vibration. We will explore how to recognize and shift lower vibrational feelings such as anger, sadness, and despair, to help raise your vibration later in the book. It is possible to move through these difficult emotions without numbing ourselves, and learning this skill is key to maintaining balance on your journey.

So, what does being stuck in negative patterns look like? This is often called 'victim consciousness', a mindset where life happens *to* you rather than *for* you. When you frequently experience emotions at the lower end of the scale, it triggers a cycle of negative thoughts and behaviours that reflect in your reality. Have you ever noticed how someone going through a tough time often faces a series of unfortunate events? The negative emotions and thoughts they carry can keep them trapped in a destructive loop. People stuck in victim consciousness often struggle with addictions as a way to escape problems they don't want to face or feel powerless to change. Their self-awareness becomes so distorted that they rewrite their story to justify how they feel. In this state, the narrative is unconsciously based on the belief that everything happening to you is beyond your control. Playing the victim card can feel like an easy way out because it avoids taking responsibility and places blame on others or life itself. However, this mindset is disempowering and restricts your ability to live life to the fullest.

The focus in healing is on shifting our emotional state with tools that help release stuck patterns and clear what's holding us back. Often, therapy work is needed to break free from this state before true progress can be made. Change begins with awareness. If you choose to stay in denial, healing through therapy can take much longer.

Awareness

In the pursuit of personal growth, awareness is the first and most essential step. It allows us to observe our thoughts, emotions, and behaviours without immediate judgement, creating the space needed to respond rather than react.

With awareness comes the ability to take a broader view. Instead of being caught up in the intensity of a single moment, we begin to zoom out and see the bigger picture. This wider perspective helps us recognize patterns over time, rather than fixating on isolated incidents. We start to notice how our present reactions are often shaped by past experiences, unspoken beliefs, or emotional wounds that haven't yet healed.

Having a broader view means we are no longer trapped in tunnel vision, where everything feels urgent or personal. We develop the capacity to pause, reflect, and ask deeper questions such as, 'Why am I reacting this way?' 'What is this moment trying to show me?' Over time, this shift allows us to move from reactivity to a more intentional response.

From this vantage point, we can hold complexity without being overwhelmed by it. We see not only our perspective but begin to understand others with more empathy. The broader view doesn't dismiss our feelings; it simply puts them in context. And with context comes clarity, choice, and the power to change.

So, how can we cultivate awareness for personal growth? Mindful practices encourage us to find and hold a focus so that our awareness is in the present. When this happens, we are fully engaged with what's going on around and within us. We become an observer, and the mind remains 'undisturbed' by what's going on in the outer world. We receive messages from our surroundings by acknowledging every single piece of information we receive through our five senses. However, the chaotic world we live in bombards us with information, making it easy for our minds to become distracted and scattered. This overload can make it difficult to focus on anything that truly requires our attention.

Another reason our awareness often drifts away from the present is because we spend much of our time caught up in the past or the future. Dandapani, a former monk and leading expert on harnessing the human mind and the power of focus, explains this beautifully in his book, *The Power of Unwavering Focus*:

> Awareness is catapulted from one area of the mind to another, driven by the carefully crafted emotional scenes of the movie, until the end is reached. The power of emotion has the magnetic force to latch onto your awareness and move it to areas of the mind associated with that emotion.[9]

According to Dandapani, awareness and mind are two different and separate things. Your awareness can move around different areas of the mind that you become conscious of, and with willpower, you can control where this awareness goes. When you are not aware, your attention is simply all over the place, travelling aimlessly around the mind, which is often led by your emotions. Worry is awareness going into the future, predicting what may or may not happen. When your awareness comes back to the present, you bring the feeling of worry with you.

The goal is to control where your awareness goes. What are you focusing on—past, present, or future? If you are present, you are not stressing over something that happened in the past, nor are you worrying about something that might happen in the future. You are simply focusing on what you are experiencing right now, which is what you have complete control over. When we can harness this technique, we can invest most of our energy into doing whatever

---

[9] Dandapani, *The Power of Unwavering Focus* (Penguin Publishing Group, 2022), 89.

it takes at this moment to create the future we desire. The present moment is what we have control of—not the past or the future.

When a past event has a high emotional charge, it has the power to pull us in, causing us to relive the experience in our thoughts. Along with this magnetic pull, frequent unconscious visits to the past make it easier for the mind to time travel, jumping back into old memories or projecting forward into imagined future scenarios. Emotional Freedom Technique (EFT), a technique that you will learn about in this book, is one of the therapeutic methods that can help reduce the emotional intensity associated with an event, so there's less chance of being dragged into the past. Once the emotional charge has dissolved, it becomes easier to stay present, as the past event is merely a distant memory.

When we carve out time every day to practise being mindful, we can quiet our thoughts and place our awareness where we want it to be—in the here and now. Awareness is something you must cultivate to navigate the process of transformation and get unstuck.

So what is self-awareness? Is it the same as awareness? Awareness involves recognizing what's happening in the present moment—acknowledging 'I'm angry'. This helps you release that anger in the moment, but it doesn't prevent the same reaction from happening again. Self-awareness goes one layer deeper. It involves reflecting on your experiences and understanding their origins and patterns—asking where the anger comes from and what's really triggering it. This is where you start connecting the dots, seeing how past experiences shape present reactions. Once you can see the root cause, you're no longer just swept along by your reactions. You begin to choose differently, and change becomes possible.

Awareness ➡ Self-awareness ➡ Self-discovery

In summary, the first step in the get-unstuck process is to cultivate awareness through daily mindful practices. These practices strengthen our ability to stay present and conscious of how we live. The next step is to develop self-awareness, which allows us to begin our inner work by reflecting on our thoughts, emotions, and behaviours. The purpose of inner work is to discover where these thoughts and emotions originate and why they continue to affect us today.

To become self-aware, we must learn how to observe our thoughts and emotions without judgement, often through meditation. This practice invites us to step back and watch our feelings as if we are watching clouds drift by in the sky, acknowledging their presence without letting them dictate our actions. For instance, when we experience emotions like anger or sadness, our natural reaction might be to criticize ourselves for feeling that way. We might think, 'I shouldn't feel this way!' But what if, instead of suppressing these emotions, we allowed ourselves to acknowledge and accept them? By doing so, we create a space for understanding.

Imagine you're feeling frustrated after a long day. Instead of pushing that feeling down, you take a moment to sit quietly and acknowledge it. You might ask yourself, 'What triggered this frustration?' and, 'Is it something I can change?' This reflection helps you to process your feelings rather than store them away, where they can fester and lead to emotional or physical symptoms later.

Learning to observe our thoughts in this way fosters compassion towards ourselves. It allows us to accept our emotions as valid experiences that contribute to our personal growth. In turn, this can lead to healthier emotional responses and a more balanced life. By embracing our emotions, we can take proactive steps to manage them effectively. Sharing our feelings with someone we trust or expressing them in a journal can be incredibly helpful. Mindfulness practices and EFT are also great tools to help us stay calm and centred. The key is to let emotions flow through us without becoming attached or passing judgement. Healthily processing our feelings regularly can prevent future complications

Intuition

The Command and Control method of parenting is an authoritative approach focused on achieving results. While often effective, it tends to overlook the child's feelings and needs, which can contribute to psychological challenges later in life. This parenting style can instil limiting beliefs in the child, such as feeling 'not good enough' and believing that love is conditional, leading them to feel they need to please others to earn love and attention. Additionally, without encouragement to develop their own intuitive and analytical thinking, the child may lose touch with their natural ability to sense what truly feels right for them.

When we depend solely on others' advice and opinions, it's easy to become confused and conflicted. Aristotle once said, 'Be a free thinker and don't accept everything you hear as truth. Be critical and evaluate what you believe in.'

Intuition is not some rare gift; everyone has it, but those who are highly intuitive learn to listen to their inner guidance instead of ignoring it. Inner conflict often starts when the way we live no longer aligns with how we truly feel deep inside. Living inauthentically is a common cause of midlife crises. We may feel disconnected and indifferent, hiding behind masks just to fit in and be accepted. Instead of embracing our authentic selves, we sometimes become ashamed of them. To get unstuck, we must learn to trust our inner voice, our inner compass, which can guide us towards freedom—a life without the limits that are imposed by a false perception of how we view the world and ourselves.

Cultivating the observer

When you become the observer of your thoughts, you give yourself space to watch them come and go, without resistance or judgement. This is a powerful shift. Instead of being caught up in your thoughts, you learn to let them pass like clouds in the sky.

Mindfulness is one of the most effective ways to declutter your mind. It helps you anchor your awareness in the present moment, rather than getting swept away by thoughts and emotions about the past or future.

When past memories surface, we often feel the emotions associated with them as if we're re-experiencing the events all over again. We might dwell on misfortunes, regrets, or wish we had done things differently. The more often these thought loops occur, the more established they become, making it easier for the mind to 'time travel'. But with consistent mindful practice, we can learn to steer our awareness and stop reliving the same emotional narratives over and over again. When a memory resurfaces, simply observe it without clinging to it and allow it to pass.

A common misconception is that mindfulness only happens during meditation. But mindfulness is, in fact, a way of living. It's about being fully aware of our thoughts, emotions, and actions in everyday life. With mindfulness, we learn to respond rather than react. We take ownership of our choices and begin to live with greater presence and responsibility. Like strengthening muscles at the gym, we can also train our minds by learning to quiet the mental noise and refocusing our attention.

Meditation is a powerful tool to help us do this. When we meditate, our minds can unwind, our bodies release stress, and our nervous systems begin to regulate. With regular practice, meditation helps us turn inwards to access the wisdom that's already there. The more overwhelmed or scattered you feel, the more meditation can support you. It gives you the space to reflect, reset, and recharge, so you can live with greater clarity and intention.

Meditation

In my morning routine, I have a set of practices that I find incredibly beneficial for preparing myself to face the day ahead. I always begin with a twenty to thirty-minute meditation to centre myself and bring calm and focus to my mind. Following that, I spend fifteen minutes in quiet reflection, writing down any insights or decisions that emerge. This practice has become a cornerstone of my day. I've found I make clearer decisions when my mind is balanced and calm.

Reflecting on my past, I remember being known as a child with a scattered mind, constantly overwhelmed by countless thoughts and lacking a sense of focus. This made it challenging to effectively harness my creative ideas, as they often remained fleeting thoughts rather than actionable inspirations. Worst of all, I struggled with mental overload and found it hard to process information. My first attempt at meditation was when I was twenty-one, but I gave up quickly after facing difficulties, concluding that 'meditation is simply not for me'—a common misconception for those with a busy mind. It wasn't until I began attending Vedanta[10] classes with my mentor that I started to embrace silence and stillness. For anyone experiencing mental congestion or depletion, I can confidently say that meditation has the power to bring clarity, balance, and a renewed sense of calm to your life.

In my experience, meditation is a profound practice that fosters a deep connection with both body and mind, helping us inhabit the present moment fully. When we practise focusing daily, it becomes easier to filter out noise and reach a non-reactive state, where thoughts and emotions no longer disturb our inner peace.

To begin meditating, start by scanning your body for any tension or discomfort. As you identify areas of unease, breathe into them and consciously release that tension on the out-breath. This

---

[10] Vedanta is one of the six classical schools of Indian philosophy, rooted in the ancient texts of the *Upanishads*. It explores the nature of reality, consciousness, and the true Self (*Atman*), which is believed to be pure, unchanging awareness. I studied within the lineage of Swami Chinmayananda, a renowned spiritual teacher who founded the Chinmaya Mission to make the timeless wisdom of Advaita Vedanta accessible to modern seekers. His teachings emphasize self-inquiry, meditation, and the practical application of spiritual knowledge in everyday life.

practice not only softens physical tension but also alleviates mental and emotional strain, contributing to your overall well-being.

Figure 4.2: Meditating to anchor the self in the present

It is common for thoughts to keep showing up, especially during stressful times. However, the objective of meditation is not to stop thoughts from arising, but to observe them without getting attached to them. You can imagine your thoughts passing by on a conveyor belt, allowing them to move along without engaging. By doing this, you begin to create space for stillness in the mind. With continued practice, you may enter a state of deep relaxation and inner peace. Your breath may feel as though it is happening at a deeper level, almost internalized.

This is a beautiful space, a timeless stillness, where everything feels calm and peaceful.

Imagine starting your day in this way, with a clean slate and a mind that is free from the clutter of recycled thoughts and emotions. By focusing on the present moment, you can dissolve stress and anxiety and cultivate a sense of inner peace and joy.

Dwelling on the past often brings regret and grief, while obsessing over the future leads to worry and anxiety. Mindful practices like meditation help us break free from these patterns, enabling us to live fully in the moment and appreciate life's richness as it unfolds.

Meditation for beginners (5–10 minutes)

Step 1: Find a comfortable seated position, either in a chair or cross-legged on the floor. Keep your spine straight, your head neutral, and your shoulders relaxed.

Step 2: Close your eyes. Take a few deep breaths—in through your nose, and out through your mouth.

Step 3: Ground yourself by noticing the weight of your body, and if seated on a chair, the contact your feet make with the ground.

Step 4: Bring your attention to your breath. Notice the movement of your body as you breathe. Pay attention to the in-breath as it enters your nostrils and fills up your lungs, then notice the out-breath as the air leaves your body through the nostrils.

Step 5: Mentally scan your body for tension. As you locate areas of tightness, breathe into those spaces and release the tension on the out-breath. If you like, you can imagine giving the tension a colour and watching it leave your body as you exhale.

Step 6: When thoughts start to come in, simply observe them and let them pass. Do not get attached to the thought. Just observe it without judgement and come back to your breath to centre yourself. Repeat this until you find complete stillness.

Step 7: When you're ready, begin to wiggle your fingers and toes. Slowly open your eyes and return to the room.

Meditation, when done correctly, helps us shift from higher to lower frequency brainwaves, moving from the faster beta state into the slower, calmer alpha and theta states, which calms the mind. Brainwaves are patterns of electrical activity occurring in the brain and are measured in frequency (hertz). There are five main types of brainwaves: gamma, beta, alpha, theta, and delta. Each corresponds to a different state of mind.

- Gamma: peak focus and heightened awareness
- Beta: the typical waking state
- Alpha: a relaxed, reflective state
- Theta: a dreamy, meditative state
- Delta: a state of deep sleep and profound healing

When we are in the beta state, our focus is on the external world. In delta, we are deeply asleep, and the mind is completely at rest.

Something powerful happens in the theta state of consciousness, when our attention turns inwards. Theta brainwaves are linked to deep relaxation, intuitive insight, and access to the subconscious mind, and it is where a lot of our inner healing and creativity come from. Alpha brainwaves, which are connected to a calm, reflective state, act as a bridge between the outer world and our inner experience. Many meditation practices help us ease into the alpha–theta range, giving us space to explore what's really going on beneath the surface—our thoughts, emotions, and patterns of behaviour.

Although most of us experience the theta state briefly while drifting off to sleep or just before waking, daily meditation and mindfulness practices can help us consciously access these brainwave states. This helps us gain greater mastery over our minds and opens a pathway into the subconscious, where beliefs are stored and impressions formed. Accessing this subconscious mind is key to shifting limiting beliefs and creating the future we desire, a space often called the field of possibilities.

Advanced meditators learn to enter alpha and theta states while awake and deeply relaxed. Beyond calming the mind and decluttering thoughts, meditation enables us to visualize and receive insights about what we wish to create. By tuning in daily, you can raise awareness, quiet your mind, reduce stress, release stored emotions, shift your perspective, tap into your creative potential, and envision opportunities aligned with your intentions and values.

Solitude

Solitude is underrated, in my opinion, and often misunderstood. My understanding of solitude is that it is a sacred space where we intentionally step away from the noise and busyness of the outside world. When we consciously choose to retreat, we give ourselves permission to slow down, turn inwards, and truly reconnect with our thoughts and emotions. Without the distractions of people or situations pulling us in different directions, solitude offers us a chance to anchor ourselves in our presence, to listen to our inner guidance, and to be truly seen and heard.

Many people are fearful of being alone as they equate being alone with loneliness. Speaking from my own experience with solitude, I can say the biggest difference is this: loneliness signals a feeling of incompleteness, while solitude is the place where you can find what you need to feel whole again.

To fully experience the benefits of solitude, it's important to turn off your phone and TV, and step away from all the 'noise'. When we weave moments of solitude into our daily lives, we open the door to profound joy and peace. If you're new to solitude, start small—perhaps with just five minutes of quiet reflection each day. Find a comfortable spot where you won't be disturbed, close your eyes, and simply breathe and connect with your breath. Over time, you might enjoy journalling your thoughts, sitting in nature, or practising gentle meditation.

Facing your shadow self

In his teachings, psychoanalyst Carl Jung used the term 'shadow self' to describe the parts of ourselves we suppress or deny. For example, someone may bury their natural emotional sensitivity after being told in childhood that showing emotion was a sign of weakness. Many empaths have experienced this, especially those who, as sensitive children, needed more care and understanding than their parents could give. Over time, that unmet need becomes a part of the self that is hidden and denied acceptance and love, particularly by caregivers. This suppression often shapes our future relationships, drawing us to familiar dynamics that feel safe on the surface, even if they limit our authentic expression. But deep down, a part of us longs to be seen and heard.

Your shadow self is not actually bad or evil; it's merely a part of who you are. We are only ashamed of this hidden part of ourselves because, since childhood, we have been conditioned to believe that some behaviours and emotions are acceptable, and some aren't. In trying to suppress or hide the parts of ourselves that don't meet these standards of acceptability, we build up layers of guilt and shame. We wear masks to be accepted, but this internal rejection prevents us from fully embracing our authentic selves. And when guilt and shame are present, they obstruct self-love and self-acceptance, keeping us disconnected from wholeness.

When we start doing shadow work, which is the essence of the healing journey, we begin to process the thoughts, feelings, and experiences that have been suppressed over the years so that we can understand ourselves at a much deeper level. Through this process, we heal old wounds and traumas and begin to relate to ourselves with more compassion and truth.

Avoiding the shadow keeps us stuck in a false narrative. To truly thrive, we must tend to the wounded warriors within us, the parts that we have abandoned. Only then can we live as our whole, integrated selves, with greater freedom, self-awareness, and peace.

Self-love and acceptance

To get unstuck, we must nurture the love necessary for the process, a love that resides within. When we let go of our inner critic and release self-judgement, we naturally return to a place of love and acceptance. As our hearts expand, the world opens up before us.

When we truly love who we are, what we do, and how we live, our perception shifts. Because we have full control over how we view events, this shift in perception has the power to change our entire experience. It really is that simple. Yet we tend to overcomplicate things—getting caught up in emotions, feeding drama, and stressing over things we can't control. This is the cycle of self-sabotage. If we want to get unstuck, we have to break it. We are often our own worst enemy when it comes to feeling stuck, but the good news is that we can choose to shift this. Every small change we make can rewire the patterns that have led us away from self-love and towards self-sabotage. We can actively choose to change our narratives.

The truth is, you become radiant when you love who you are. Your energy glows, and it lights up the room. People respond to how you feel about yourself; they can sense the shift. Yet many of us wait for external validation to determine how we feel inside. We tie our self-worth to how others perceive us. But when you let go of the need for approval, you take back your power. You choose how you feel every single day.

Self-love is not selfish. In fact, it's a deeply selfless act because when you stop relying on others to fill your cup, you show up more authentically in your relationships without any hidden agendas. You can only truly love others when your own cup is full. And as you carry this loving energy, you naturally attract people who resonate with it or those who are inspired by it because it's what they've been seeking.

Reflection (journalling prompts)

My daughter loves asking the question, 'Why?' and she doesn't stop asking until I run out of answers. Like many children, her curious mind wants to get to the root of everything. The question, 'Why?' stems from their curiosity about the world and is their way of seeking answers about what they are experiencing. We too can ask 'why' to get to the real essence of every situation, followed by 'what' to find a solution.

I like asking, 'Why?' when I'm in a meditative state, with a calm mind that remains neutral. Understanding the reasons behind past events is crucial for getting unstuck: Why was I unhappy? Why did I feel and think that way? Why is it still affecting me now? Then come the 'what' questions: What adjustments need to be made to change this? What new emotions and thoughts would I like to have to feel unstuck? What needs to be done for me to move forward from this?

To get ourselves unstuck, we must first look at the stuckness within us, in both body and mind. This means taking a moment to pause and reflect on how we truly feel. Once we bring that into balance, our outer reality will naturally start to change in response to how we feel internally.

The Power Is Within You

Each morning, you can choose to live your best life. Too often, our routines put us on autopilot, dulling our awareness and keeping us stuck in familiar patterns. When we live unconsciously, we miss the small miracles and possibilities around us. Instead, we let things outside us trigger reactions that knock us off balance. We find ourselves trying to prove our worth or control what happens, often because we are afraid that if we show who we really are, we won't be accepted or feel enough. This fear keeps us hiding behind masks and stuck in patterns that drain our energy. Instead of letting your environment control how you feel, you can choose joy and freedom from within. The power to shape your day and your life is in your hands.

Just like in *The Matrix*, when Neo is offered the choice between the blue pill—to return to the comfort of the familiar—or the red pill, to face the truth and step into the unknown, you too have a choice. You have the power to decide whether to take the key that unlocks the door leading to freedom on the other side of change.

The decision is yours alone.

Part II

Your Guide to Emotions

'Hurt feelings don't vanish on their own.
They don't heal themselves.
If we don't express our emotions, they pile up like a debt
that will eventually come due.'

—Marc Brackett

5

When Our Emotions Are Out of Whack

I have always been fascinated by the study of emotions. I feel things deeply, not only my own emotions, but also those of others. This high level of sensitivity, once perceived by others (and even by me) as a weakness, has turned out to be one of my greatest strengths. Over the years, I have come to understand how my sensitivity and intuition work together to help others acknowledge and process their emotions. I guide them to see where those feelings come from, what messages they carry, and how they can be used as catalysts for change.

Emotions are not inconveniences to suppress or ignore; they are signals. When we stop dismissing or avoiding them and start understanding their purpose, we unlock a powerful source of information. Emotions can serve as powerful guides on the path of self-discovery and healing, if we're willing to listen.

How We Respond to the World Emotionally

The limbic system, often referred to as the emotional brain, is made up of a group of structures that govern how we feel and respond emotionally. Two important parts of this system are the amygdala and the hippocampus. The amygdala is responsible for detecting threats and activating our fight-or-flight response, while the hippocampus helps us process and store emotional memories.

When we feel stressed or unsafe, the amygdala kicks in, signalling the body to prepare for survival by releasing stress hormones like cortisol and adrenaline. This response is hardwired into all mammals, but unlike animals, we humans can activate this response just by thinking. A memory, a worry, or even an imagined scenario can be enough to trigger the same survival mechanisms as if we were in real danger.

The problem is that many of us live in this reactive state without realizing it. We replay past events, anticipate the worst, and stay mentally 'on guard', unknowingly keeping our nervous systems stuck in high alert. Over time, this can feel like our default setting, and we become so used to the tension that we don't even notice it. Our stress responses become automatic. We overreact, take things personally, and lose perspective.

Daniel Goleman, author of *Emotional Intelligence: Why It Can Matter More Than IQ*,[11] explains this process as an 'amygdala hijack'. When strong emotions flood in, the amygdala takes over before our thinking brain, the neocortex, has time to make sense of what's happening. This is why we sometimes say or do things we later regret. In those moments, we are not being rational, we are simply reacting from a place of emotional overwhelm.

How Can We Prevent an Amygdala Hijack?

As well as using meditation and mindful practices to calm the mind and become less attached to our emotions, it's also important to understand why we get triggered in the first place. Emotional triggers are often signs of unresolved issues that stem from painful

[11] Daniel Goleman, *Emotional Intelligence: Why It Can Matter More Than IQ* (Bloomsbury, 2009), chapter 2, eBook.

or traumatic experiences—events that felt overwhelming at the time and shaped the way we see the world. A traumatic experience is any situation that causes intense distress or fear, overwhelming our thoughts, emotions, and nervous system. Its impact depends on the emotional intensity it provoked and the severity of the event itself, and the resources available to us at the time. When we have the support that we need to process what happened, trauma has less lasting impact than when we face it alone.

Trauma can arise from many situations, such as the loss of a job, a breakup, or being in an abusive environment. But it can also stem from moments that might seem insignificant to an outsider. Imagine a five-year-old proudly showing their drawing to a parent who, distracted and tired, says, 'Not now, I'm busy.' To the child, this might feel like proof that what they create isn't good enough, or that they're not important. These early interpretations become the lens through which we see ourselves and the world. Your work here is to gently explore how these experiences may have influenced your beliefs, shaped your worldview, and led you to form certain vows or survival patterns that once protected you but may now be holding you back.

When we find ourselves triggered by someone's words or actions, our immediate reaction is often to blame them or wish they had acted differently. For instance, a friend might cancel plans at the last minute, a colleague could overlook your contributions, or a loved one might say something hurtful. In those moments, it can feel as though the issue lies entirely outside of us. However, what if the real story is unfolding within? The truth is, it's rarely just about the other person. Their actions merely reflect unresolved wounds, unmet needs, or hidden fears within us that are yearning for acknowledgement. Each difficult interaction serves as an invitation, not to fix or blame the external, but to turn inwards and ask, 'Why is this happening for me now?' and, 'What part of me needs healing?'

By viewing challenges through this lens, we reclaim our power. Instead of perpetuating old cycles, we can utilize these moments as opportunities for healing, growth, and evolution into a more conscious and authentic self. This self responds from a place of presence rather than reaction, holds compassion for its wounds, and navigates life with clarity and courage.

One of the most powerful tools I use to help release stuck emotions and support the brain's natural ability to rewire itself is Emotional Freedom Techniques (EFT), also known as tapping. EFT was developed in the 1990s by Gary Craig, a Stanford engineering graduate, who combined elements of ancient Chinese acupressure with modern psychology. This simple yet effective practice involves tapping on specific points along the body's energy meridians while focusing on the emotions or sensations we want to heal. The process helps calm the nervous system, reduce emotional intensity, and restore balance to the body's natural energy flow while also supporting the brain in forming new, healthier associations. With time, tapping can shift deeply ingrained beliefs and emotional blocks that keep us stuck, making it an essential part of the healing journey.

When using tapping to heal unresolved trauma, we begin by focusing on an emotion or physical sensation while tapping on the meridian points. Unlike traditional talk therapy, the story (how the event unfolded) is not the crucial part of the protocol. My clients often notice a series of related past events arising in their minds during the tapping sequence. Tapping sends safety signals to the brain, allowing past events to be reprocessed and stored in a more neutral way. By doing this, we can reduce the intensity of the related emotions as they surface with the memories. Once we have completely dissolved the emotional intensity of the earliest event associated with the emotions, the perception of subsequent events can be shifted. By retrieving the past emotions, we tap and clear away whatever remains within our systems until we experience a 'cognitive shift', when our perception of the event completely changes. This shift in perception allows us to see things in a positive light as we release the negative emotions attached to the event that shaped our beliefs and the way we perceive the world.

Tapping's effectiveness depends on our willingness to let go of the emotions we're holding onto. When we resist, we prevent the shift from happening by clinging to what we believe, even though it hurts to remain in this space. This resistance stops the safety signal from fully overriding the old alarm response in the brain, which means the brain can't completely reprocess the memory into a calm, neutral state. The mind seeks familiarity; whatever feels familiar is where it feels safe. For any kind of healing to be beneficial, we must feel safe enough to receive it with an open mind and allow the process to take place gradually. Patience is the key to healing, and impatience is one of the most common barriers to healing and growth.

Emotional Memory and Patterns

Beyond its role in triggering the fight-or-flight response, the amygdala helps with processing and encoding emotionally charged memories, especially those linked to fear, pain, or threat. Early life experiences such as abandonment or rejection can create lasting emotional patterns in the brain. While these memories are not stored as logical facts but as emotional impressions, they involve complex networks including the amygdala, hippocampus, and other regions that influence how we respond to similar situations later in life.

When a current experience resembles one of these past wounds, such as someone pulling away, ignoring you, or changing their tone, the amygdala responds as if the original threat is happening all over again. This is why emotional reactions can feel overwhelming and out of proportion to what's actually happening. It's not that you're being dramatic, it's your brain trying to protect you from feeling that same pain again.

Gradually, these emotional patterns become embedded as protective mechanisms. They are your brain's way of helping you avoid similar pain in the future. However, because the amygdala responds rapidly to threat cues without waiting for full contextual processing, these protective reactions can be triggered even when the current situation isn't truly dangerous, leading to overreactions, shutdowns, anxiety, or even self-sabotage.

For instance, if someone cancels plans or doesn't reply to a message, you might spiral into feelings of rejection, not because of the current situation itself, but because it echoes a past experience your emotional brain has flagged as dangerous. Recognizing when this is happening helps you separate the past from the present and choose a new way forward.

Intuition and Gut Reaction

Intuition is a common term in the wellness community, but it's crucial to understand how it differs from a gut reaction. Let's explore this distinction.

You've probably heard people talk about following your head, your heart, or your gut. While we have one brain in our head, our heart and gut also have their own neural networks that communicate with our brain. Your head is where logical thinking happens. Your heart responds to and influences your emotions. And your gut, with its extensive nervous system, is connected to your most primal instincts about safety and danger.

These three centres communicate through the autonomic nervous system, with the vagus nerve acting as the main channel linking them. When stress hits, the vagus nerve helps activate the parasympathetic nervous system to bring us back to balance.

It's no surprise then that we feel butterflies in our stomach when nervous or experience digestive issues under chronic stress. Our gut nervous system is closely tied to the limbic system, including the amygdala, which responds to past experiences and sends signals, our gut instincts that warn us of potential threats. This gut reaction is primal, aimed at survival.

Dr John Demartini, a renowned human behaviour specialist and author, offers a framework for understanding this difference. He explains that what we often refer to as a gut instinct is actually a response from the amygdala and the enteric nervous system. It pushes us either towards something (an impulse) or away from something (an instinct), both of which are rooted in survival mode. In contrast, intuition arises from what he calls the 'thrival state'. Studies show that when our heart rhythms, brain, and nervous system are synchronized, we experience enhanced clarity and better intuitive discernment.[12] In this integrated state, the prefrontal cortex, the thinking brain, works in harmony with the heart. This state brings inspired knowing: a deep sense of certainty that isn't driven by logic or emotional impulse.[13]

Understanding this difference is important. Gut reactions are driven by emotions and past conditioning, often focused on avoiding pain or danger. Intuition, however, guides us towards growth and aligned action. When all three centres are connected and balanced, we feel grounded, clear, and aligned. Tuning into this thriving, intuitive state allows us to pause before reacting (based on past experiences) and instead take inspired actions that support our well-being. Have you ever just known something felt right without being able to explain why? That's your intuition speaking.

---

[12] 'Science of the Heart: Exploring the Role of the Heart in Human Performance,' Research, HeartMath Institute, https://www.heartmath.org/research/science-of-the-heart/energetic-communication/

[13] John Demartini. *The Breakthrough Experience: A Revolutionary New Approach to Personal Transformation* (Hay House, 2009).

It's important to note that intuition-led actions can sometimes feel like impulsive decisions. They can arise in an instant, like seeing a signal and immediately responding to it, without analysing it with your logical mind. The difference between what I call a 'download' and a reactive decision is that the former comes from a place of certainty and clarity, whereas the latter feels urgent, protective, and preventative, like a knee-jerk moment. This is because a reaction is ultimately driven by fear.

You can learn to differentiate between the two by becoming more aware of these impulses and when they show up for you. Notice how you feel in the moment—what are you doing, thinking, and feeling? The most common reference to this is when people say their best ideas come in the shower or just after waking up. Both examples highlight how we access our intuitive faculty when the body and mind are relaxed.

Recognizing the source of our inner guidance helps us make better decisions and live more authentically, moving beyond survival and into thriving.

Coming Out of Survival Mode

The autonomic nervous system consists of two divisions: the sympathetic nervous system and the parasympathetic nervous system. The former helps you enter fight-or-flight mode when under threat, and the latter helps you exit it. The system gets out of balance when the fight-or-flight response is triggered frequently, meaning anything we experience that makes us feel stressed or unsafe can kick-start the stress response process and cause us to act impulsively and instinctively.

An effective way to regulate this is to stimulate the vagus nerve so the parasympathetic nervous system kicks in, allowing the body to rest, digest, recover, and heal. The vagus nerve, which runs from the brainstem to the gut, acts like a communication channel between the brain and the body. When stimulated, it helps switch off the stress response and brings the nervous system back into balance. This is called increasing vagal tone, which is linked to better emotional regulation, greater resilience to stress, and improved physical health.

There are many ways to stimulate the vagus nerve and boost vagal tone. These include slow, deep belly breathing, somatic practices that help you tune into and release tension in your body, cold exposure like cold showers or contrast (hot and cold) therapy, and practices such as humming, chanting, and singing, which use vocal vibrations to stimulate the vagus nerve. Yoga, especially gentle or mindful styles, and meditation also help calm the nervous system and support vagal tone.

The key to coming out of survival is learning how to feel safe again. If our nervous system doesn't believe we are safe, it will keep us in survival mode, hyper-vigilant, guarded, and emotionally reactive, even when the threat has long passed.

Living in survival mode can feel like you are constantly on edge, overstimulated and anxious, as if your body is always bracing for something to go wrong. It's a state where fight, flight, or freeze becomes your default, not just a short-term response. While this way of being may have served a purpose in the past, perhaps during a difficult childhood, a toxic relationship, or an overwhelming life phase, it can become so deeply ingrained that it becomes your normal state of being.

Coming out of survival begins with awareness. We cannot shift what we haven't yet acknowledged. When we start noticing how we react, whether through people-pleasing, over-functioning, shutting down, or avoiding discomfort, we begin to interrupt the pattern. It's important to approach these behaviours with compassion. These were survival strategies and coping mechanisms that helped us feel safe when we didn't. Rather than criticizing and judging ourselves for being 'too sensitive' or 'too much', we can meet these parts of us with understanding and ask: What is this reaction protecting me from? Where did I learn that I had to respond this way to be safe or accepted?

Our job now is to show the nervous system that it's safe to be here. Safe to slow down. Safe to rest. Safe to feel. This is where tools like EFT tapping, breathwork, and meditation come in, not as quick fixes, but as consistent practices to regulate the nervous system, recalibrate the body, and rewire the brain. These practices help us anchor back into the present and gradually build a sense of safety.

Transitioning from survival mode to what I call creative mode feels like moving from constriction to expansion. We stop reacting out of fear or past wounds and begin responding from a place of clarity, curiosity, and possibility, the beginner's mind, as mentioned earlier. In this state, we are open to new perspectives and present to what's here, rather than locked into past narratives. The body relaxes. The mind opens. The heart becomes more available. This is where transformation happens, by allowing ourselves to feel safe enough to be who we truly are. When we feel safe enough in our own skin, we no longer need to perform, protect, or prove. We can simply be. And that's where real change begins.

6

Emotional Health

As we saw earlier, the vagus nerve plays a crucial role in helping our body shift out of stress and back into balance. Emotions are not just passing feelings; they are deeply connected to how our bodies function. Positive emotions encourage relaxation and healing, while negative emotions like fear activate the body's stress response.

Stress hormones released during fight-or-flight are meant for short bursts, but today's constant pressures often keep us stuck in chronic stress, making it harder for our bodies to reset. When emotions aren't fully processed, the body can remain in a heightened state of alertness, keeping us overwhelmed and reactive. This ongoing stress affects not only how we respond to life but also our physical health, weakening the immune system and increasing vulnerability to illness.

In his book, *When the Body Says No*, Dr Gabor Maté explores the connection between chronic stress, emotional repression, and disease. He notes that 'repression of anger is not an abstract emotional trait that mysteriously leads to disease. It is a major risk factor because it increases psychological stress on the organism'.[14]

Most stress management programmes only target the aftermath of this situation by managing the stress rather than finding its root

[14] Maté, *When the Body Says No*.

cause and making radical changes that would have a lasting effect. If your stress and the problems it causes stem from emotions that are being ignored and suppressed, that means emotions are the key to unlocking your stress cycles. To get unstuck, you have to master your emotions—not just by practising positive affirmations, but also by healing the parts of you where past emotions are stored.

In his book, *Letting Go: The Pathway of Surrender*, David R. Hawkins, a spiritual teacher and author known for his work on consciousness and emotional healing, discusses the ways we handle our feelings:[15]

1. **Suppression and repression**
   While repression happens unconsciously, suppression is a conscious choice. In my experience, people often use both as ways to avoid dealing with difficult emotions by sweeping them under the carpet. Toxic positivity—the push to practice positive affirmations without processing real pain or feelings can contribute to this. We consciously jump from negative to positive, leaving emotions unmetabolized and trapped in our system. Repression is often driven by fear. According to Hawkins, 'Of these mechanisms used by the mind to keep the feeling repressed, denial and projection are perhaps the best-known methods, as they tend to go together and reinforce each other.' In other words, instead of allowing ourselves to feel and accept our emotions, we deny or project them onto others. We avoid taking responsibility and create false narratives to justify our thoughts and behaviours. This keeps us stuck in low-vibrational emotions like anger, shame, resentment,

[15] David R. Hawkins, *Letting Go: The Pathway of Surrender* (Hay House, 2018), 11–15.

guilt, and fear. The longer we stay in this state, the more disconnected we become from reality.

2. **Expression**
   Expression involves venting or showing feelings through body language or actions, rather than denying them. Hawkins explains that expressing negative feelings lets out just enough pressure so the rest can be suppressed again. So, even though we express emotions, we may not actually release or let go of them. The emotions continue to control our thoughts and behaviours, and expressing them can sometimes reinforce their validity, making it harder to move past them. This can lead to reactive behaviours, where we project toxic feelings onto others instead of taking responsibility for them.

3. **Escape**
   Escape is the avoidance of feelings through diversion, and it is the most common coping mechanism. Hawkins points out that avoidance underlies many addictions to alcohol, drugs, work, and other distractions, which momentarily help us avoid our feelings. He explains, 'The projection of these repressed feelings results in social problems, disorders, and the increase of selfishness and callousness characteristic of our present society. Most of all, the effect is the inability to truly love and trust another person, which results in emotional isolation and self-hatred.' Escapism leads to emotional numbness, where we distract ourselves until we feel nothing. The problem is, staying numb requires constant activity, such as excessive phone use, working, shopping, overeating, partying, and so on. Ultimately, what we're escaping from is often ourselves. When we are still and quiet, we can't avoid our own company, and those who struggle with being alone

might need to ask why. Healing is the only way out of this cycle of emotional numbness.

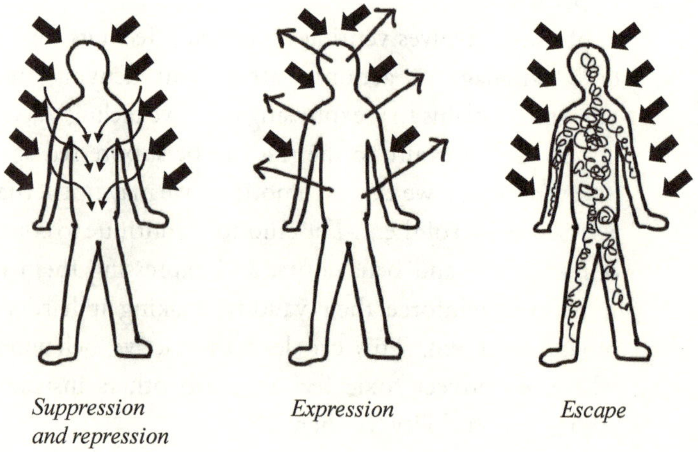

Figure 6.1: Ways we handle feelings

Using Emotions as a Healing Guide

When we feel physical pain, we usually monitor it for a while before deciding to seek professional help, especially if it doesn't go away or begins to interfere with our daily life. If we are under the weather, we might take a day off to rest. Many of us rely on home remedies or over-the-counter medications for something like a cold or an upset stomach. And if those don't help, or we are too unwell to function, we know it's time to consult a doctor. On some level, we all understand that if the body begins to shut down, it's a sign to get help. But when it comes to emotional or mental distress, the warning signs are often ignored, sometimes until it's too late.

Let's consider emotional pain, which is deeply connected to mental well-being. When we're in deep emotional pain, do we ask for support? Although society has made progress in destigmatizing mental health, there is still a great deal of shame around needing emotional help. As Brené Brown notes, this shame often stems from our difficulty in embracing vulnerability.[16]

Being 'emotional' is still commonly misunderstood as a flaw or weakness. We have all heard things like: 'Why are you so emotional?' or, 'You're overreacting.' Many of us were raised to suppress our feelings, avoid big emotional displays, and just carry on. Women have often been judged as too emotional to lead, while men have been conditioned not to show emotions at all, associating any display with weakness. For generations, we've been taught to sweep feelings under the rug and power through. But have you ever wondered why the emotions are there in the first place?

Our emotions play a huge role in how we experience everyday life. They are not here to punish us, they are here to guide us. When we learn how to work with our emotions, by acknowledging, accepting, and releasing them, we loosen their grip on our behaviour and well-being.

Acknowledge ➡ Accept ➡ Release

It's important to recognize that emotional healing can be intense and, at times, deeply uncomfortable. Real healing work often brings old pain to the surface, and we must be willing to sit with it. When we start to see pain as a teacher, we open the door to healing with less resistance. This is at the heart of emotional processing: allowing pain to surface, not to re-live it endlessly, but to acknowledge it, accept it, and release it for good.

When we continue to suppress or store painful emotions, they can create imbalances in our mental and physical health. If we want to live a life of balance, vitality, and joy, we must clear out the toxic emotional residue. Healing isn't about bypassing what we feel; it's

---

[16] Brown, *Daring Greatly*.

about making space for something better to take root. So, what does it actually mean to release something?

In healing spaces, we often hear phrases like 'let it go', 'release what no longer serves you', and 'set yourself free'. However, true release begins with perspective. It involves not taking things personally, which can be particularly challenging when we are in pain. By stepping back, we can reflect on the situation through a broader lens. Instead of fixating on how we were wronged or what others did to us, we begin to understand both sides and the emotional dynamics at play. With this clarity, we can start to let go, freeing ourselves from the burden of our experiences.

Letting Go: The Path to Emotional Freedom

Letting go isn't just a mindset, it's an emotional shift. It is the moment we stop clinging to past pain, stories, or identities that no longer reflect who we are becoming. While reflection helps us understand the emotional charge behind a situation, letting go is what releases it from our system. And that release doesn't happen all at once; it's something we return to again and again. Every time we are triggered, we are being invited to release just a little more of what has been weighing us down.

Letting go doesn't mean pretending the past didn't happen; it means choosing not to carry its emotional weight into the present. It's about allowing the past to remain behind us, preventing it from distorting our view of the present or shaping our reactions to the future.

Letting go is not a one-time decision but a continuous practice of loosening our grip on the stories, pain, and behaviours formed from earlier experiences. Oftentimes, when we are triggered or feel intense emotional discomfort, we are not just reacting to the moment at hand, but to everything it reminds us of. When we feel misunderstood, unsafe, judged, abandoned, or that life is unfair, those emotions usually echo much older wounds, some of which we may not even consciously remember.

When we don't let go, we amplify. The emotions fester, intensify, and eventually shape our beliefs about ourselves, others, and the world. That's why people often overreact under stress; the reaction isn't really about what is happening right now. It is the emotional build-up of everything that came before that felt similar.

There are generally two ways people attempt to let go. The first is to walk away from the situation or the people involved. They cut ties, block phone numbers, or bury the event without ever examining it. But this isn't true letting go; it's avoidance. When we skip the reflection, we miss the lesson. We might feel relief for a while, but the same emotional patterns will likely resurface in the next situation that touches that same wound. What we need to let go of is our reaction to the situation. And that can only happen through reflection and ownership. It begins with asking:

- What did this stir up in me?
- What is the repeated pattern here?
- What part of me was activated and why?
- What is this situation inviting me to see or learn about myself?

The first step is not taking it so personally. That doesn't mean denying your feelings; it means creating just enough emotional distance to see the fuller picture. Once we stop looping in victimhood or blame, we can consider the other person's perspective. This doesn't excuse harmful behaviour, but it gives us room to understand the emotional dynamics at play. With that awareness, we can then ask: How do I want to show up next time?

Letting go is about accepting what happened, taking the insight from the experience, and choosing not to carry it forward with bitterness or resentment.

Letting go is an ongoing process towards liberation. It requires presence, honesty, and a willingness to revisit the layers when they resurface. But each time we do, we soften and reclaim a little more of our energy. As David R. Hawkins writes: 'Surrender is a constant process of not resisting or clinging to what the mind thinks it wants or fears.'[17]

Letting go doesn't mean forgetting. It means being free.

Emotional Detox

Many people understand the benefits of a body detox, but emotional detox is still unfamiliar to many. When we overindulge, our bodies experience indigestion and don't have enough time to properly process the food we have eaten. This affects our system's optimal functioning and can leave us feeling sluggish. Similarly, our emotional well-being can experience its own form of 'indigestion', an emotional overwhelm, commonly known as burnout. When emotions are unprocessed and pent up, they can create blockages that disrupt our inner balance. As time goes on, this emotional accumulation can contribute to chronic stress, anxiety, physical discomfort, and even illness.

Emotional detox is the process of routinely checking in with ourselves, reflecting on our thoughts and emotions to prevent that internal backlog. This might include self-healing practices like journalling, tapping, breathwork, and meditation. For deeper or more intense emotional experiences, seeking help from therapists, coaches, mentors, or energy healing practitioners can be incredibly supportive. Sometimes we need someone to hold space for us in order to process what we are carrying. The goal is to create safe and healthy ways for repressed emotions to surface and be released. This

---

[17] Hawkins, *Letting Go*, 42.

helps us reset emotionally, carry less baggage, and ultimately feel lighter and more grounded.

Participating in group healing experiences like support groups or healing circles can also be profoundly impactful. These spaces offer a sense of belonging, connection, and emotional safety, which is vital when working through vulnerability. Engaging with others who share similar struggles fosters mutual trust and empathy. That shared energy helps cultivate a spirit of community where we feel seen, heard, and supported.

Taking Accountability

Emotional detox helps us process and release past emotions that would otherwise become stuck in our systems. The pivotal moment of healing is when we make ourselves accountable for our behaviours and repeated patterns. When we feel hurt, it is easy to fall into victimhood and place the blame on others. Accountability means taking responsibility for the consequences of our choices and taking complete ownership of our responses to them. Looking inwards rather than outwards is the key to making a long-lasting change in how we experience life.

When we feel we have been mistreated, it is easy to give our power away by focusing on the other person's behaviour and how small it makes us feel. However, how others treat us does not define who we are; it is often a reflection of their own inner struggles, burdens we are not meant to carry.

Rather than feeling betrayed or disrespected, take a step back and adopt a broader view of the situation. Hurt people hurt others. The moment we choose not to take it personally we free ourselves from emotional entanglement. We begin to see our patterns, such as allowing such behaviour in the first place. By making ourselves accountable, we create significant change by making necessary adjustments and breaking our behavioural patterns.

Part III

Getting Unstuck

'My father taught me that you can read a hundred books on wisdom and write a hundred books on wisdom, but unless you apply what you learned then its only words on a page. Life is not lived with intentions, but action.'

—Shannon Alder

7

Heal

'Three routes to healing:
1. You must let the pain visit.
2. You must allow it to teach you.
3. You must not allow it to overstay.'

—Ijeoma Umebinyuo

I love this quote by Nigerian poet, Ijeoma Umebinyuo. It is a simple yet relevant breakdown of what healing entails, which forms the first stage of the UNSTUCK framework.

Healing for Emotional Balance

In the UNSTUCK framework, 'heal' refers to the inner healing that brings the body and mind into a state of balance and well-being across all levels. Through this healing, we begin to change the patterns that have kept us out of alignment, by observing and shifting stuck emotions and removing limiting beliefs that have kept us trapped in old cycles. This is the most crucial part of the programme, as it lays the foundation for creating a new reality, a new way of living. It is essential to master our emotions when it comes to getting unstuck.

In energy healing, we work with the understanding that our presence, thoughts and emotions create an exchange between us and others. According to research by the HeartMath Institute[18], our thoughts produce measurable electrical activity in the brain, while our emotional states influence the electromagnetic field generated by the heart. This field can be detected several feet away from the body and is thought to play a key role in how we affect and are affected by our environment.

Energy-sensitive individuals, such as empaths or healers, often describe their ability to perceive this field and interpret emotional states based on it. Simply put, the more positive our emotions, the higher our vibration, and that energy is contagious. You can feel it when someone walks into a room with grounded confidence or genuine warmth; it naturally draws others in. When we consistently embody this kind of presence, we become magnetic in a subtle and authentic way, allowing people to feel safe and drawn to that energy.

It is clear that healing is an important part of our journey and that healing creates space for us to become our best selves. However, there are some negative preconceptions and myths about healing, causing reluctance in people from proudly pursuing it. A few examples of such myths are:

- Healing is only for people who are emotionally damaged.
- Just think positive thoughts and you will be healed.
- Healing is a 'woo-woo' thing to do.
- Focusing on emotions and feelings is self-indulgent.
- A healer or therapist can take away your pain.

---

18 'Science of the Heart: Exploring the Role of the Heart in Human Performance,' Research, HeartMath Institute, https://www.heartmath.org/research/science-of-the-heart/energetic-communication/

- Once you're healed, you'll never experience negative emotions again.
- An alternative to healing is simply pushing through. Why open Pandora's box when the past is already behind you?

Many people hold misconceptions about what healing entails. There is an unspoken fear that seeking help signifies weakness. In my experience, the opposite is true. Healing is not for the faint-hearted; it requires courage to face unhealed wounds and honesty to confront the parts of ourselves we have buried. Revisiting the past can be deeply uncomfortable, which is why many people avoid it. However, those unprocessed emotions do not disappear; they remain lodged in our nervous system, quietly driving our behaviours and reactions.

Eventually, we become more reactive, overwhelmed by emotional clutter and burdened with false beliefs. So, we must ask ourselves: would you rather remain stuck, feeling unloved, uninspired, and disconnected, or endure temporary discomfort to reclaim a life that feels whole, purposeful, and free?

I can tell you from experience that the reward is worth it. There is nothing more liberating than restoring your authentic self. By releasing what no longer serves you, you find peace and make room for new, meaningful experiences. Even if the process is challenging, simply seeing things clearly and no longer living under old illusions or inherited beliefs is a breakthrough in itself. Sometimes, the truth alone is enough to begin the get-unstuck journey.

Understanding Trauma and the Inner Child

Many of us have encountered some form of trauma in childhood. A common misconception is that trauma must be dramatic or life-threatening. In truth, trauma can be subtle—a moment of feeling abandoned when lost in a supermarket at the age of five can also leave an emotional imprint. That unhealed fear or loneliness may follow us into adulthood. Healing often involves reconnecting with the inner child, fostering self-love, and learning to accept ourselves unconditionally. This is vital for reframing negative thinking, dissolving limiting beliefs, and embracing our authentic nature.

Trauma doesn't only stem from abuse or neglect; it can also result from emotional needs that weren't met. A child who feels unheard or unseen may grow into an adult who constantly seeks validation. This sets the stage for unhealthy relationship dynamics, where we are repeatedly drawn to situations that confirm our core wounding.

Unresolved trauma leads to reactions to perceived threats from the past, and these emotional triggers keep us in survival mode, constantly scanning for danger and feeling stuck in fear. This ongoing stress distorts our perspective and limits our ability to thrive, and can, ultimately, push individuals to their breaking point. However, it doesn't have to be this way.

If you, like me, are yearning for a more peaceful and balanced life, this is your invitation to begin the healing journey. We all carry unresolved wounds; acknowledging their presence is the first step. That moment of awareness is the spark that begins your transformation and marks the start of your return to wholeness.

Listening to the Signals

A few years ago, an ongoing back pain that started after childbirth was causing me so much agony that it began to hinder my yoga practice and disrupt my sleep. It appeared as a dull, persistent ache in my lower back, which I became accustomed to until a yoga master told me the pain was in my mind, not my body. I decided to look deeper and, through healing, uncovered the emotional root of the pain. With both physical training and mental adjustments, the pain eventually subsided, and thankfully, it never returned. That was when I realized that change begins when we listen to our pain instead of pushing it aside.

Pain, whether physical or emotional, is always legitimate. It's a signal that something within us needs attention, but emotional pain is often overlooked. We have learned to compartmentalize, to keep going, to get on with things. The problem is, what we ignore doesn't disappear. It stays with us, often surfacing through the body in the form of tension, fatigue, or pain. Unprocessed emotions can linger in the nervous system, quietly influencing how we feel and respond, until we are ready to listen.[19]

Our emotions can guide us to liberation. We feel them when triggered, pointing to wounds that need healing. Just as we seek help for physical injuries, emotional pain deserves similar care. Many of us were raised to downplay our feelings, leading to disconnection and suppression, until our bodies insist, 'No more.'

In healing, we often describe the journey as peeling back the layers of an onion. This means letting go of false beliefs, protective patterns, and outdated stories. With each layer released, we come closer to the truth of who we are. At the centre is our most authentic self, waiting to be remembered.

Understanding the Onion Effect

Before we can shift and rewire our beliefs, we must first recognize how profoundly they shape our identity and how significantly they are influenced by societal expectations and judgements. For instance, does having a university degree guarantee success? Not always. Similarly, does being unmarried or childless by thirty-five signify failure? Again, not necessarily. Judging our actions as right or wrong places us in a realm of comparison and criticism,

---

[19] Bessel van der Kolk, *The Body Keeps the Score: Brain, Mind, and Body in the Healing of Trauma* (Penguin Publishing Group, 2014).

compelling us to make decisions based on how others might perceive us. Consequently, we often end up emotionally punishing ourselves when we don't conform to societal expectations.

We convince ourselves we are not good enough simply because we don't fit the standards set by others. Our inner critic constantly reminds us of our supposed flaws and imperfections. This state of being is a form of self-sabotage that only leads to misery and distress. It is time to flip the script, silence that inner critic, release limiting beliefs, upgrade our belief system, and start living the life we truly want.

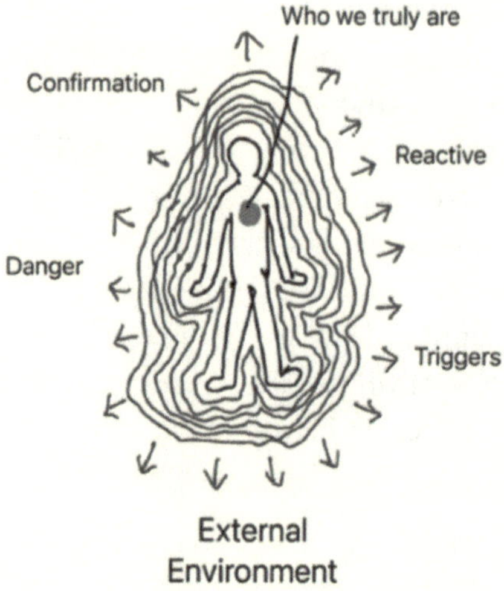

Figure 7.1: The onion effect

In the onion effect diagram, the layers represent our emotional responses and perceptions formed from past experiences—the thoughts, emotions, and behaviours we developed during childhood. This is the emotional baggage we carry and the survival strategies we learned. It is often said that a child's mind is like a sponge when it comes to learning.

Dr Joe Dispenza, a doctor of chiropractic and expert in neuroscience and personal transformation, explains that children's brainwaves are predominantly in the theta state between the ages of two and six. During this time, the subconscious mind is highly impressionable and receptive to new information, absorbing it without critical analysis, since the analytical mind doesn't fully develop until around age twelve. As we develop the capacity for critical thinking, we begin to question and filter information. Before this develops, we accept everything we see and hear as truth. These formative years are when our beliefs get conditioned, shaping how we view the world as adults.[20]

In EFT tapping and other healing modalities, we often guide clients back to their childhood, usually before age seven, to uncover and remove the root cause of limiting beliefs. This is when our core belief system, the 'programme' by which we live, is established. Once set, it governs how we interpret experiences and shapes our reality, constantly reinforced over time.

Conflict arises when we sense that our programmed beliefs don't truly resonate with our authentic selves. Despite this inner knowing, our logical mind insists these beliefs are valid due to past experiences. Ignoring this inner voice can lead to feelings of being stuck by the time we reach thirty. This internal tug-of-war continues as our true self nudges us towards change, while our inner critic, formed by childhood experiences, demands we remain safe and comfortable. This critic, laden with judgement and criticism, aims to protect us from further hurt by keeping us in familiar situations. Negative self-talk, such as 'I'm not good enough' or 'I don't have what it takes' traps us and blocks our growth.

Comfort is often our greatest enemy. When we feel too settled with how we live, growth becomes impossible. The only way to get unstuck is by stepping out of our comfort zones. We can do this by silencing that inner critic and living in alignment with our true beliefs, values, and purpose. When we tune into our bodies

---

[20] Joe Dispenza, *You Are the Placebo: Making Your Mind Matter* (Hay House, 2014), chapters 1–3.

and connect with our hearts, we can feel the emotions that arise as we reflect on the past experiences that hold us back. As mentioned previously, repeating the same habits and behavioural patterns keeps us trapped in the old narrative, preventing us from stepping into the unknown where new possibilities await. When our daily lives become too predictable and repetitive, it is a clear sign that we are stuck in our comfort zone.

Stepping out of our comfort zone can be challenging but it is crucial for personal growth. Life is a series of obstacles, and with each one we overcome, the next becomes easier. Change is often intimidating and uncertain, so it's natural to feel uncomfortable in unfamiliar situations.

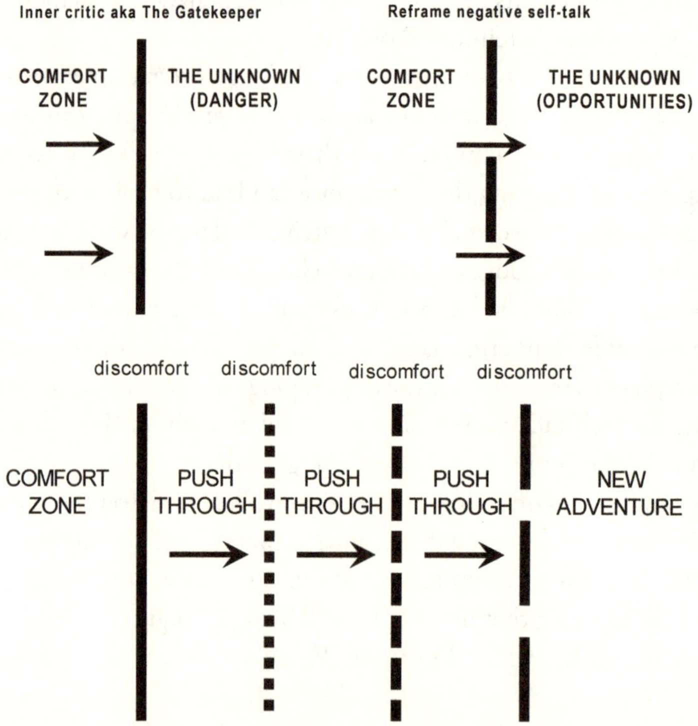

Figure 7.2: Discomfort barriers

Instead of fearing change, try leaning into curiosity and excitement. Remember the beginner's mind we talked about earlier—that fresh, open way of seeing things without judgement. Approaching change with this mindset transforms it from something scary into an adventure. It helps us welcome new possibilities with openness rather than resistance and enables us to push through mental barriers. With patience and perseverance, lasting change is within reach for all of us.

Embracing Vulnerability

Despite what we have been taught, we are not meant to be happy, high-functioning, and emotionally bulletproof all the time. Healing asks us to create space for all parts of ourselves, including the messy and painful ones. It's about learning to feel our feelings without judging them or pushing them away. When you allow yourself to cry after a stressful day or feel the sting of a painful memory, you are not breaking down; you are processing. Crying activates the parasympathetic nervous system, which helps soothe the body and regulate the nervous system. It is one of the ways we naturally release tension and come back to a state of balance.

Vulnerability can also show up when we feel hurt or disappointed by a friend, a partner, a parent, or a boss. Letting those feelings be seen gives us access to the wound underneath. That is where the real healing happens. Eventually, you start recognizing emotional patterns for what they are, rather than reacting on autopilot. You learn to observe your feelings instead of suppressing or bypassing them. Think of emotions like water—always moving, always changing. This metaphor isn't meant to be a scientific statement, it is meant to help explain how emotions work. If we let emotions flow, they eventually settle. But if we hold them back or try to bottle them up, they build pressure. Left unprocessed, those stuck emotions can turn into chronic tension, anxiety, or fatigue.

So yes, let the tears fall. There is nothing weak about feeling deeply; it is your body's way of processing and healing. When we stop resisting our emotions, we begin to shift. When we stop resisting what we feel, we can start moving again.

Rewriting the Programme (aka the Belief System)

A big part of healing is becoming aware of the beliefs we have carried, especially the ones that were never really ours to begin with. Many of our beliefs get formed in childhood, shaped by how we were raised, what was praised, and what was punished. If a child learns that love is earned through achievement or that expressing feelings gets them shut down, they take these learnings as messages that then dictate their behaviour and form their core beliefs. These messages don't just go away. They become part of the internal programming, the subconscious beliefs that shape how we see ourselves and how we move through the world.

Fast forward to adulthood, and we often find ourselves stuck in the same loops. Maybe we overwork ourselves to prove we are worthy. Maybe we choose the 'safe' path instead of the one we truly want, only to end up burned out or resentful. And when things don't go as planned, it is easy to fall back into those old, familiar thoughts: *I'm not good enough. I always mess things up. I should've known better.*

Understanding the past is helpful, but insight alone isn't always enough to shift the emotional charge. That's because a lot of this programming lives in the subconscious and the body, not just in the thinking mind. Neuroscience confirms that implicit memories (memories outside of conscious awareness) can continue influencing our behaviour long after the event is over.

Peter's Story

Let me share a story about one of my clients. I have changed his name to protect his privacy, but his experience is a powerful example of how our inner programming can shape the course of our lives, often without us even realizing it.

Peter is in his thirties, a father of three, and by most standards, he is doing exceptionally well. He is the CEO of a thriving company, lives in a beautifully designed home, drives a luxury car, and takes his family on overseas holidays every couple of months. His life appears to be one of success and balance. He's admired in his professional circles and deeply devoted to his children. On the surface, he seems to have it all. But beneath that polished exterior, there is a subtle sense of discontent that he can't quite explain. A feeling that something is missing.

Peter grew up in an affluent environment with very strict parents. His childhood was predominantly shaped by constant assessments of how well he was performing at school and whether he was meeting the high expectations set by his family. 'There is always room for improvement no matter how well I'm doing,' became his mantra. As a child, this pressure caused subtle but persistent anxiety, driven by fears of disappointing others and beliefs such as 'it's never enough' or 'I'm not good enough'.

Fast forward three decades, and Peter still carries those beliefs. He has learned to suppress his emotions, cope by staying busy, and project strength and resilience at all times. It is what he believes a CEO and a father should do. His emotional pain, often stemming from childhood, is buried beneath a high level of performance and a tightly managed life. He rarely stops to acknowledge how he is really feeling. When he does, it is usually late at night during brief moments of stillness when the noise dies down and the sadness creeps in. He logically understands that his parents were doing what they thought was best for him. He knows they wanted him to succeed, but the body keeps the score, and no amount of intellectualizing can erase the emotional imprints left behind. When Peter faces adversity, that deeply ingrained belief of 'I'm not good enough', flares up and activates his stress response.

He might snap at a colleague when he feels undermined or withdraw from his spouse when he's told he isn't doing enough at home. On the outside, it looks like he is managing. But on the inside, he is running on autopilot, driven by old beliefs that no longer serve him. His coping mechanisms? Numbing with alcohol, staying busy, pushing through. They are keeping him functional, yes, but not fulfilled. His body has started to speak in other ways too—persistent aches, fatigue, and stress-related symptoms that medication only manages temporarily. Nevertheless, the deeper root cause remains untouched.

As Dr Bruce H. Lipton explains:

> The conscious mind is the 'self,' the voice of our own thoughts. It can have great visions and plans for a future filled with love, health, happiness, and prosperity. But whilst we focus our consciousness on happy thoughts, who is running the show? The subconscious. And it's running it precisely the way it was programmed.[21]

What this means is that no matter how much Peter might want a joyful and connected life, his subconscious is still running the outdated software of his childhood—scripts like, 'Don't mess up', 'You must perform,' and, 'You're only worthy when you achieve.'

Lipton's work, particularly *The Biology of Belief*, shows that the biggest barriers to realizing our dreams often come from limitations programmed into the subconscious mind. These deeply ingrained beliefs not only shape our behaviour but can also influence our physical health.

So, while Peter's conscious mind desires a joyful and connected life, his subconscious mind is still operating from a place of fear and self-protection. These are fundamentally out of alignment, and until the inner programming is addressed and rebalanced, the outer success will always feel slightly incomplete.

---

21 Lipton, *The Biology of Belief.*

Gabor Maté describes the 'controlling personality' as an obsessive coping style that arises from unmet childhood needs. In our quest for safety, we often attempt to control every detail of our lives. However, true safety does not stem from control; it is rooted in healing, and a return to wholeness.

Emotional Freedom Technique (EFT): Tapping

As EFT tapping was introduced earlier in the book, here I'll focus on how I use tapping within the UNSTUCK framework to heal past trauma and reframe old experiences.

EFT tapping works by gently stimulating specific points on your face and body, the same acupoints used in acupuncture for thousands of years. What's fascinating is that science is now beginning to understand what ancient practitioners knew intuitively. These acupoints correspond to what's called the primo vascular system, a network of microscopic channels running through your body's connective tissue.

When you tap on these points, the physical pressure creates electrical signals through a process called mechanosensory transduction. In simpler terms, you're sending calming signals directly to your brain—particularly to the amygdala, which acts as your emotional control centre. Research by Dr Peta Stapleton, a clinical and health psychologist and leading researcher in EFT at Bond University in Australia, has shown that these signals help soothe your stress response from within by deactivating the amygdala while you're focusing on distressing thoughts or memories.

The reason this works comes down to how our bodies conduct electricity. Acupoints have lower electrical resistance than the surrounding tissue, and when you tap, you generate what's called piezo-electric energy. Your body's collagen acts as a conductor, transmitting these signals along the primo vascular pathways to your brain. This is why EFT is often described as 'acupuncture without needles', both work with the same system, just using different approaches.

When stress or trauma disrupts your system, your nervous system can become stuck in fight-or-flight mode. What makes EFT so effective is how quickly it can shift you out of this heightened state. Even without following a rigid script, tapping becomes a powerful and effective self-soothing tool. It deactivates your sympathetic nervous system and allows your parasympathetic state, your body's natural 'rest and digest' mode to take over. This is where genuine healing can occur. [22]

When working through past events in EFT tapping sessions, the focus is less on the details of the story and more on processing the emotions and physical sensations involved. We rate emotional intensity on a scale from 0 to 10, and as we tap on meridian points, the trapped emotions begin to dissolve. Combined with elements of cognitive therapy, exposure techniques, and somatic stimulation, EFT helps to clear emotional intensity by fostering acceptance and release.

The goal in one-to-one EFT tapping sessions is to uncover the root cause of recurring emotional patterns and systematically process the emotional charge held in those memories. When we identify core events using techniques like the 'movie title technique' or 'tell the story', we work through each aspect and detail while tapping, allowing the trapped emotions to release. This deeper work allows us to stop unconsciously replaying old dramas. The brain's capacity for neuroplasticity means we can reprogramme our neurological pathways to shift limiting beliefs and behaviours. By tapping to

[22] If you'd like to explore the science more deeply, Dr Stapleton's research provides extensive documentation on how tapping affects both the primo vascular system and brain function. See: Peta Stapleton, 'The Latest Science of Clinical EFT Tapping,' virtual lecture, posted June 19, 2023, by Dr Peta Stapleton, YouTube, https://youtu.be/GMa6Dv4OUrc

reduce emotional intensity, our logical mind naturally reframes perspectives that were previously overridden by emotion.

In practice, a typical EFT tapping session involves:

1. Client brings an issue
2. Support client in finding emotions and body sensations associated with the issue
3. Use that information to find earlier times when they felt the same things
4. Use EFT techniques to dissolve emotional intensity of these core events
5. Identify limiting beliefs
6. Tap directly on the beliefs or allow reframing to occur naturally and in subsequent sessions, explore additional memories supporting that belief to fully release it
7. Restore calm

In group sessions, I guide participants through generalized tapping scripts to neutralize surface-level emotions and bring calm. For deeper trauma, working with a certified practitioner is essential to ensure safety and effectiveness.

Tapping steps

Step 1: Think of an issue that is bothering you.
Example: *I am feeling anxious about an upcoming event.*
Measure how the issue makes you feel by rating it on a scale of 0 to 10, with 10 being the most intense.

Step 2: While gently tapping on karate chop (side of hand) point (see below diagram) with the fingers of your other hand (can use more than just two), set up a statement for your issue that begins with 'even though' and ends with 'I deeply and completely love and accept myself'.

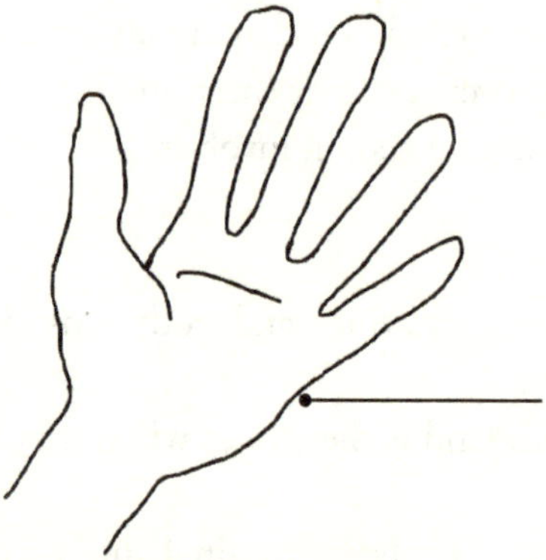

Figure 7.3: Karate chop/side of hand point for the set-up statement

Example: *Even though I feel anxious about the work event next week, I feel nervous and apprehensive. I deeply and completely love and accept myself.*

Step 3: Start tapping on the rest of the meridian points on your face and body by following the sequence below. While you tap, use reminder phrase, i.e. anxious about the work event next week, and highlight the emotions or body sensations that you are feeling.

Step 4: Tap until your discomfort level is down to 0. This can take three to four rounds, depending on the intensity. Once you feel the intensity of the emotions has dissipated, you can finish by making a positive affirmation such as 'I am safe', 'I am calm', or 'I am relaxed' to complete the sequence.

What if the intensity doesn't go down or goes up?

If your number stays the same or increases after a few rounds of tapping, this often means:

- You've uncovered a deeper aspect of the issue that needs attention. For example, 'anxiety about the work event' might reveal underlying feelings like 'fear of being judged' or 'worry about making a mistake'. Adjust your setup statement to address this new aspect and continue tapping.
- The issue might be too general. Try being more specific about what's bothering you. Instead of 'anxious about the work event', narrow it down to 'anxious about speaking in front of my boss' or 'worried I'll forget what to say'.
- There's a physical sensation demanding attention. If you notice tension, tightness, or discomfort in your body, tap directly on that: 'Even though I have this tightness in my chest . . .'

If you feel overwhelmed or your intensity continues to rise after several rounds, pause and ground yourself:

- Stop tapping and open your eyes. Look around and notice five things you can see in your present surroundings.
- Take slow, deep breath—breathe in for a count of four, hold for four, exhale for four.
- Feel your feet on the floor or your body in the chair. Notice the physical sensations of being supported.
- Place a hand on your chest or heart and remind yourself: 'I am safe right now. I am in the present moment.'

If you're dealing with traumatic experiences or deeply distressing issues that feel too difficult to handle on your own, seek support from a qualified EFT practitioner who can provide the guidance to navigate these deeper issues safely.

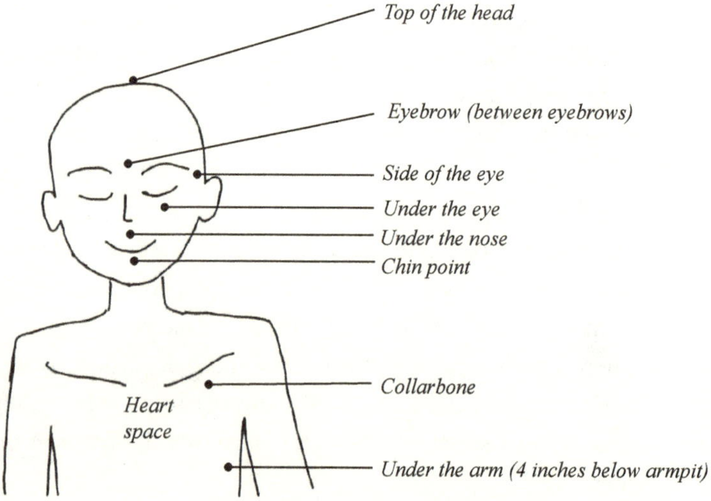

Figure 7.4: Tapping points

Tapping script for anxiety and stress

Before we begin, take a deep breath and tune into your body. Close your eyes and bring your awareness inwards. Feel the soles of your feet where they make contact with the floor. Ground yourself fully. Rate the intensity of how anxious and stressed you feel on a scale of 0 to 10. Start tapping gently on the karate chop point for the set-up statement:

- *Even though I'm feeling anxious, I honour how I feel and I give myself permission to relax.*
- *Even though I feel this anxiety in my body, I am open to complete relaxation.*
- *Even though I feel this tension all over my body (or name a specific area that is bothering you), I honour how I feel and give my mind and body permission to completely relax.*

Round 1

Top of the head:

All this anxiety.

Eyebrow:

I notice it in my body.

Side of the eye:

I notice the heaviness of this emotion.

Under the eye:

All this anxiety in my [name a specific part of your body where it feels tight].

Under the nose:

It's so hard to relax with everything that's going on.

Chin point:

I feel the weight all over my body.

Collarbone:

[Acknowledge the main reason for feeling anxious. For example, 'I have so many deadlines,' or 'Everything is happening all at once.']

Under the arm:

I find it so hard to relax. I feel exhausted.

Round 2

Top of the head:

[Think about the reason and notice any emotions rising to the surface; then tap on these emotions.]

Eyebrow:

I choose to let go of all these emotions so I can relax.

Side of the eye:

I choose to release [name the emotions]. I am ready.

Under the eye:

I am ready to let go of these emotions.

Under the nose:

It's okay to relax.

Chin point:

It's safe to relax.

Collarbone:

Right now, I am safe. I don't need to have all the answers right now.

Under the arm:

I can begin to let go and choose peace instead.

Tap on heart space (thymus):

Releasing all the tension as I allow my body to completely relax.

After completing the tapping sequence, take a moment to place your hands over your chest to seal in the energy. Then, rate the intensity of your emotions again on a scale from 0 to 10. Notice any changes or shifts in how you feel. If your discomfort hasn't lowered to zero or to a level you find manageable, simply repeat the tapping rounds as needed. There's no rush, allow yourself to move through the process at your own pace. When you feel calm and relaxed, take a few deep breaths into your heart space and appreciate the stillness you have created. When ready, end the practice by saying, 'Transform.'[23]

Moving Through Loss

It can be challenging to cope with endings, especially when they are unexpected. The habits and routines we establish in familiar

---

23 'Transform' originates from the work of Peter Donn, UK (an EFT Master Trainer), who since 2003 has been developing a set of subconscious-level healing instructions intended to be 'executed' by the higher self. The command 'transform' is used to release or transform felt emotions or feelings and is often used within or after an EFT tapping sequence to increase efficacy. He has given the author permission to use and share it in its current form in this book.

situations often feel out of place when circumstances shift. Change can be extremely difficult to comprehend. Remembering the times when we used to go to work and have lunch with colleagues after leaving a job can bring up feelings of sadness and longing. Matters of the heart, such as the end of a relationship, can be even more difficult to process. Emotions like betrayal, regret, anger, and resentment may linger if we don't take the time to acknowledge and release them. To break free from this cycle of negative thoughts, we need to be fully aware when memories resurface and trigger past emotions, causing us to relive those experiences repeatedly, much like a relentless nightmare.

Shifting our focus to the present can help us avoid getting lost in those memories. Meditation can increase self-awareness and enable us to become more conscious of our thought patterns. By cultivating the ability to return our awareness to our breath and body, we can interrupt the replay of distressing memories. With consistent practice, we can train our minds to dwell less on the past and remain grounded in the present.

EFT tapping can help reduce the emotional intensity associated with revisiting painful memories. By acknowledging, accepting, and releasing negative emotions, we create a distance between past events and our present experiences. It is important to give ourselves permission to feel, process, and let go of these emotions in healthy ways, so they don't become buried and unresolved.

Dealing with loss is an incredibly personal journey, and emotional processing is crucial in navigating this challenging experience. This can involve a range of practices, such as talking to trusted friends or therapists, journalling to express and make sense of thoughts, tapping to calm the nervous system, meditation to centre the mind, and breathwork to regulate emotions and ease tension.

Loss is a natural part of life, whether it is the loss of a job, a relationship, a loved one, or a particular lifestyle. It is essential to navigate the grieving process to fully accept and let go of what has been lost. Grieving allows you to create emotional closure. The duration of the grieving process can vary significantly, taking days, months, or even years, depending on the depth of the loss. Without closure, unresolved thoughts and emotions can become trapped in the mind and body.

Reflection ➡ Realization ➡ Redirection

Reflection helps you process the past. Realization allows you to extract meaning from your experiences, and redirection enables you to let go of what no longer serves you so that you can move forward. Giving yourself time and patience to transition into something new is essential when closing a chapter of your life. I have found tapping to be a powerful way to process grief. However, many therapeutic methods can help support you through the stages of grieving. Grieving can be incredibly tough, especially when we feel deeply attached to what we are losing. This is likely why so many people turn to distraction or replacement.

Grieving often requires solitude, but it can also be supported through safe connection. The key is to observe the pain and discomfort, acknowledge it before it can dissolve and release. Many people with unprocessed trauma develop unhealthy coping mechanisms to avoid pain—such as numbing, avoidance, or over-functioning. These tactics may offer temporary relief, but they only delay healing. The pain doesn't disappear; your body holds on to emotional memories whether you are aware of them or not. If you are experiencing physical issues or recurring symptoms, it may be your body signalling an emotional blockage that needs to be resolved. This is why emotional healing is such an important part of restoring balance in the mind, body, and soul.

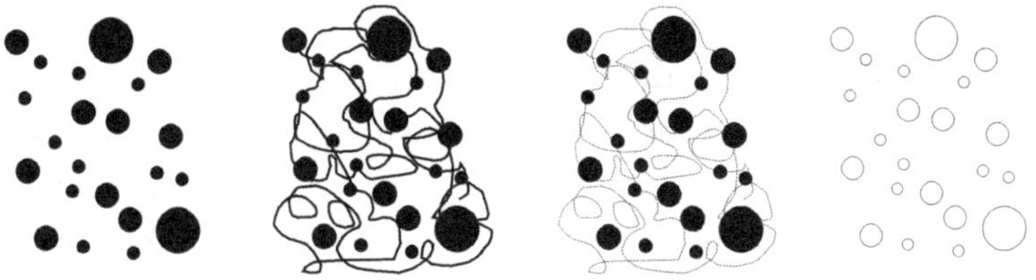

Figure 7.5: The grieving process

The grieving process is unique to each individual; there is no one-size-fits-all approach. While some may find solace and self-heal, others might struggle to cope with loss or the end of something significant. Recognizing when you need support is crucial, and seeking professional help can be invaluable. Having someone to hold space for you and guide you through this challenging time can make a significant difference, especially when it feels difficult to detach from your emotions and regulate them.

Always remember that 'this too shall pass'. (I say this based on my own experience of grieving.) No matter how intensely painful it feels to let the emotions come through, nothing in this world lasts forever, and time really does heal. Every moment you spend processing what arises during grief helps to lessen the emotional intensity that is attached to the story. Be gentle and compassionate with yourself. Give yourself full permission to grieve, to be vulnerable, and to find closure. Take time out for as long as you need to regroup and reset. Your future self will thank you for it one day.

Forgiveness

It was only recently that I felt I had begun to forgive and let go completely, something that typically unfolds during or after the grieving stage. The most common resistance to forgiveness is the belief that doing so lets someone off the hook. In my case, years of what felt like emotional abuse had led me to maintain a narrative of being a victim. In truth, I had unconsciously held onto this role to validate the pain I had endured, which stemmed from someone else's unresolved trauma and coping mechanisms. But by holding onto this narrative, I was unable to free myself emotionally. I realized that by choosing not to forgive or forget, the only person I was hurting was myself.

The grieving process allowed me to dissolve enough of the emotional charge tied to the past that I could begin to see things with greater clarity. As I gradually detached from the intensity of those emotions, a wave of compassion and understanding washed over me. That is when I knew I could begin to truly forgive and let go.

What makes this process so complex is that forgiveness must extend not only to the other person but also to ourselves. Typically, we direct anger outwards when deep down, we are most angry or disappointed with ourselves, for what we tolerated, what we didn't see, or what we couldn't change. On top of that, the drive to fight for justice can feel empowering but may actually mask deeper feelings of fear or pain. What feels like strength—our determination to rebuild and move forward, can sometimes be a survival response to not feeling safe.

Sometimes, forgiveness opens the door to another layer of grief. You may find that there are still others to forgive, or that you haven't fully forgiven yourself. This stage is intricate and can take months or even years, depending on the depth of the wound and the resistance you feel. The first step is to surrender and allow yourself to be vulnerable. Only then can you begin to soften and release the anger that is buried deep within.

When we consciously choose to view a situation with a willingness to forgive, we begin to loosen the emotional bonds tied to the event and the people involved.

Anger is often the hardest emotion to release, especially when we feel betrayed, dismissed, or wronged. It is intense and tends to amplify with every trigger. In EFT tapping, unresolved anger is a common block to healing, making it difficult for the emotional intensity to truly dissolve. If there is someone you need to forgive, the forgiveness exercises in this book can guide you to release and neutralize these heavy emotions. The more painful the experience, the harder it is to forgive those who caused harm. For those who have experienced abusive or life-threatening trauma, I strongly recommend working with a trauma-informed professional to support the healing process in a safe, guided way.

Louise Hay, a renowned author and teacher on emotional healing, writes in her book *You Can Heal Your Life* about how feeling stuck often means there is still room for forgiveness. She explains that when we do not feel we are living in flow, it indicates we are holding onto the past.[24] If you are determined to get yourself unstuck, forgiveness is a significant step that cannot be missed.

When we forgive ourselves and others, we release the emotional tether that keeps pulling us back into the same old story. In doing so, we create space for something new to emerge.

UNSTUCK Toolbox for Heal

Boundary setting

There are six primary types of personal boundaries: emotional, physical, sexual, intellectual, material, and time. Personal boundaries are the invisible lines that help us define where we end and others begin. They protect our energy, time, emotions, and values which are vital for our well-being, especially during seasons of change or healing. Most of us instinctively grasp physical

24 Louise Hay, *You Can Heal Your Life* (Hay House,1984).

boundaries; for example, when someone stands too close in a public space, we may step back to regain our comfort and safety. This personal space allows for harmonious coexistence with others. In contrast, emotional boundaries are often less tangible and more challenging to navigate.

Emotional boundaries define our ability to separate our feelings from those of others. When these boundaries become blurred, we can unknowingly absorb others' emotions, resulting in stress, anxiety, and burnout. By establishing clear emotional boundaries, we can safeguard our mental well-being and cultivate healthier relationships.

A common challenge arises when we feel compelled to help or fix others' problems, often at the expense of our own needs. While this impulse may come from a good place, it can lead to co-dependency, where our self-worth becomes intertwined with our ability to care for others. By establishing healthier boundaries, we can support others without enabling harmful behaviours. This means offering presence without overfunctioning—holding space with empathy, rather than overextending ourselves to shield others from the consequences of their actions. In relationships, be it with partners, children, or friends, it is crucial to recognize when we are overstepping our limits. By stepping back from the urge to overprotect, we create space for more authentic, balanced, and respectful connections.

Another indicator of boundary issues is becoming entangled in others' drama. In our fast-paced world, unnecessary emotional involvement can be draining. Many people, often unconsciously, are drawn to drama and then wonder why they feel exhausted. When our energy is consumed by matters that don't serve us, we have little left for what truly matters.

In today's digital age, boundaries are easily crossed online. Whether it is oversharing on social media or allowing others' curated lives to affect our self-esteem, the digital world can blur the lines of personal boundaries. Teenagers and young adults, in particular, are vulnerable to these influences, leading to issues like imposter syndrome and diminished self-worth, so it's important for parents and adults to model healthy digital boundaries. When we model discernment, we empower younger generations to do the same.

Setting healthy boundaries is especially vital during periods of personal transformation. As we work to get unstuck from old patterns, we must be mindful of the people we surround ourselves with. Some relationships may no longer align with our evolving values and goals. It's okay to distance ourselves from those who hinder our growth, even if it's challenging. This space allows for new, more supportive connections to form. As you become more attuned to your needs and set healthier boundaries, your social circle may naturally shrink, and that's completely normal. This isn't about becoming isolated; it's about creating space for relationships that truly support your well-being. Sometimes, as individuals grow and evolve, paths may diverge. However, it is also possible for connections to rekindle if both parties find their journeys aligning once again.

Being nice at the expense of your truth is not kindness; it is self-betrayal. Many of us are conditioned to believe that being 'nice' means prioritizing others' needs over our own and fearing rejection or conflict. This self-sacrificing behaviour can lead to resentment and burnout. True kindness, which is different from merely being 'nice', involves honouring our own needs and boundaries while treating others with respect. By cultivating self-love and authenticity, we can form deeper, more genuine connections that support mutual growth and understanding.

Rest and recovery

The 'hustle culture' of recent years makes it difficult to sustain a well-balanced lifestyle. The constant need to do and achieve more means our bodies and minds do not get the chance to reset and recharge fully. When we don't allow our bodies to carry out their natural balancing and healing processes, we eventually reach a point where they stop functioning properly. This can lead to mental and physical exhaustion—a burnout.

People who suffer from stress and anxiety often find it hard to switch off at night. In more extreme cases, some experience regular insomnia. Tapping is very effective for regulating stressful emotions and preparing the body for rest. You can use the script below every night as part of your bedtime routine to prepare yourself for better sleep.

Nadi suddhi pranayama

This is a simple alternate nostril breathing technique that can bring calmness to the body and mind as we focus on our breathing. In this practice, we start and finish with the left nostril—this is intentional, as the left nostril is linked to the ida nadi, which activates the parasympathetic nervous system, promoting rest, relaxation, and emotional balance. It is a gentle way to activate calm energy and wind down, especially before bed.

1. Sit in a comfortable position and close your eyes.
2. Rest your left hand on your left knee. You can place your hand palm facing up in chin *mudra* (thumb and index finger gently touching) if that feels comfortable or simply rest it in a relaxed position.
3. Bring your right hand to your face. Fold your index and middle fingers towards your palm.
4. Use your right thumb to close your right nostril.
5. Inhale slowly through the left nostril.
6. Close the left nostril with your ring finger, then release the right nostril.

7. Exhale slowly through the right nostril.
8. Inhale through the right nostril.
9. Close the right nostril again with your thumb and release the left nostril.
10. Exhale through the left nostril.

This completes one cycle.

Repeat this sequence for five to ten minutes. Always complete the practice with an exhale through the left nostril.

Energy healing

Energy healing includes modalities such as singing bowl therapy, EFT tapping, acupuncture, BodyTalk, Reiki, and chakra-balancing, which can help bring the body and mind back into balance. Group sessions are great for general clean-up and rebalancing; however, it is best to work privately with a certified practitioner for more intensive work. We can also incorporate energy healing into our daily lives to align the body and mind at the start of the day.

Here's the backstory to my healing journey. After my health scare in 2016, I chanced upon a singing bowl gallery and bought my first singing bowl. Since then, I have used a singing bowl every morning as part of my meditation practice. Its effect prompted me to get certified as a singing bowl therapist so I could help others experience the benefits of sound healing. This daily practice gradually introduced me to the deeper world of energy healing, particularly the *chakra* system, a key framework for understanding how energy moves within the body.

Energy healing is deeply connected to the chakra system, an ancient model of seven main energy centres in the body. Each chakra corresponds to specific physical, emotional, and spiritual aspects of our being. In energy healing traditions, when these energy centres are balanced and flowing freely, this is associated with optimal health and well-being. However, stress, trauma, or negative experiences are believed to create blockages in our chakras. This is where energy healing comes in. Practices like singing bowl therapy, EFT tapping, Reiki, or acupuncture aim to clear these blockages and restore the natural flow of energy through our chakras. For instance, the vibrations of a singing bowl can help activate and harmonise specific chakras, promoting healing on multiple levels. By working with the chakra system through various energy healing modalities, we can address both physical and emotional imbalances, leading to a more harmonious and balanced life.

Chakra balancing

Chakras are subtle energy centres believed to be linked to the nervous and endocrine systems. They were first described as centres of consciousness in ancient Indian scriptures such as the *Upanishads*. When in balance, these energy centres, often visualized as spinning wheels, bring harmony to our physical, emotional, and spiritual health.

According to the traditional chakra system, chakras can be open, closed, or imbalanced to varying degrees, and their condition can shift throughout life in response to circumstances and unresolved emotions. A blocked chakra is believed to disrupt energy flow, showing up as physical symptoms or emotional patterns. When our chakras are aligned, our feelings and thoughts sync with our actions and communication.

Fear is an emotion that all human beings experience throughout life, often stemming from unresolved childhood experiences. Unmet childhood needs can turn into coping mechanisms that make us feel safe but may block the energy flow in the system, leading to imbalance. In chakra healing, fear is associated with the root chakra, and when left unaddressed, it can manifest as physical symptoms such as lower back pain, digestive issues, and insomnia.

Regular self-check-ins can help you notice emotional and physical cues from your body. Stuckness in life can reflect a disruption in your energetic system. Practices used for chakra-balancing, such as sound healing, visualization, movement, or breath can help you reconnect with what needs healing and return to balance. These techniques have been shown to support for stress reduction and emotional well-being.

The chakra system offers a perspective on energy and well-being, widely embraced in many holistic healing practices. While chakras aren't scientifically proven, many people find this approach helpful in making sense of the connection between mind, body, and subtle energy.[25] In chakra healing traditions, imbalances are believed to correspond with the following physical and emotional patterns. Physical symptoms should always be evaluated by a qualified healthcare provider, as these associations reflect traditional teachings rather than medical diagnoses.

Below is an overview of how chakra imbalances may contribute to the feeling of being stuck.

- **Root chakra**
  Fear of change, lack of safety and security
  - This chakra governs our sense of stability and belonging. Resistance to change can block this centre, keeping us in survival mode. When balanced, we feel grounded, confident, and safe to move forward.
  - Physical symptoms: Lower back pain, leg issues, fatigue, or problems with the colon or immune system.

[25] Subtle energy refers to a non-physical form of energy described in many ancient healing traditions, including *Ayurveda*, Traditional Chinese Medicine, and Reiki. While it cannot be measured by conventional scientific instruments, it is often used in holistic and energy-based practices to describe sensations, emotional states, or spiritual awareness.

- **Sacral chakra**
  Suppressed emotions, blocked creativity
  - This centre governs creativity, sexuality, and emotional flow. Guilt, shame, or unprocessed emotions can cause imbalance.
  - Physical symptoms: Hip pain, reproductive issues, urinary tract problems, lower abdominal discomfort.
- **Solar plexus chakra**
  Lack of self-esteem and motivation
  - This is the seat of our personal power and will. When blocked, we may procrastinate or feel powerless. When balanced, we take decisive action with confidence.
  - Physical symptoms: Digestive problems, liver or pancreas issues, adrenal fatigue.
- **Heart chakra**
  Lack of self-love or difficulty in relationships
  - This centre bridges the physical and spiritual. Unresolved grief, betrayal, or self-criticism can close it down. When open, we feel love, compassion, and connection.
  - Physical symptoms: Heart and lung issues, chest pain, upper back tension, immune disorders.
- **Throat chakra**
  Fear of expressing your truth
  - This chakra is linked to authentic communication. It may be underactive (difficulty expressing) or overactive (dominating speech). Balance here helps us speak and listen with clarity and confidence.
  - Physical symptoms: Sore throat, thyroid imbalance, jaw tension, neck stiffness.
- **Third eye chakra**
  Lack of clarity, disconnection from intuition

  - This centre governs insight, intuition, and imagination. Over-reliance on logic or the need for control can block it.
  - Physical symptoms: Headaches, problems with eyes and sinuses, poor focus, insomnia.
- **Crown chakra**
  Disconnection from meaning or spiritual guidance
  - This chakra represents our connection to the divine or higher self. It can feel blocked during existential crises or periods of disconnection.
  - Physical symptoms: Migraines, dizziness, sensitivity to light or sound, chronic fatigue.

There are many ways to work with your chakras, such as meditation, yoga, crystals, sound healing, and energy work. Incorporating these into your daily life can support your overall well-being and help you feel more grounded, empowered, and in flow.

When our chakra system is in balance, many people report:

- Feeling safe and secure to pursue their dreams (root chakra)
- Expressing their creative ideas with ease (sacral chakra)
- Acting with confidence and clarity (solar plexus chakra)
- Making decisions from a place of love and compassion (heart chakra)
- Communicating with authenticity (throat chakra)
- Trusting their inner wisdom (third eye chakra)
- Feeling divinely connected and guided (crown chakra)

While chakra healing can support emotional and energetic well-being, it's important to listen to your body and seek medical care when needed. For many, working with chakras complements other forms of healing and offers helpful insights into the mind–body connection.

If you are curious to explore chakra healing in greater depth, I recommend *Wheels of Life: A User's Guide to the Chakra System* by Anodea Judith. It's a classic reference that combines psychology, spirituality, and energy medicine in an accessible and practical way.

Reflective journalling

Writing down and processing our thoughts and emotions serves as a valuable tool for self-reflection and personal growth. By maintaining a reflective journal, we can gain a clearer understanding of how to move forward positively. Reflecting on our daily experiences allows us to recognize the patterns and habits that shape our lives.

Self-reflection is not about replaying past events; it is more like doing detective work in a mindful state to gain new insights about a situation. This should not be confused with rumination, where thoughts become negatively obsessive, eventually leading to stress and anxiety.

When we are in self-reflective mode, we become observers rather than experiencers, which allows us to analyse a situation without judgement. It doesn't trigger negative self-talk or create stress. Most importantly, the process is not meant to be repeated. When you begin to overthink or overanalyse a situation, you know you are not reflecting but mulling over it obsessively. The goal is not to replay and re-experience past events, but to reflect on what you have gained from the experience and how you can make improvements.

Shifting from, 'Why is this happening to me?' to, 'What is this trying to teach me?' can profoundly alter our perspective. By viewing a situation through this lens, we empower ourselves to learn and grow, transforming feelings of disempowerment into empowerment. Everything happens for a reason; there are no coincidences. When we start to reflect on past experiences and their impact, we can take steps to create a better outcome in the future. When we don't give ourselves enough quiet time to reflect and decompress, we can't review and learn from the past and make better choices.

The key to reflection is to hold yourself accountable for the decisions you make and the actions you take. While we can't always control what happens to us, we can take responsibility for how we respond and the meaning we choose to create from our experiences. You have always had more power than you may have realised, and each moment gives you a new opportunity to respond differently and create change. Choose to act as if you are 100 per cent responsible for everything that contributes to your happiness. If something doesn't turn out as planned, you can ask yourself these questions:

- What did I do or not do to create this result?
- Why did I respond the way I did?
- How am I feeling now?
- Are these emotions something I have felt in the past?
- What can I do to neutralize these emotions?
- What can I do differently next time?

If you keep repeating the same responses to life events, you will keep getting the same result. The day you change your response is the day your life will begin to change. Give up blaming others, take charge of your life, and work out how you can change your thoughts, emotions, and behaviours to get a different result. A good way to start the self-reflective process is to begin with a breathing exercise to calm the mind and then use the journal prompts mentioned above to reflect on your day.

Journalling and tapping for emotional clarity

Find a quiet place where you can completely relax and be alone and undisturbed for thirty minutes. Once you are in a comfortable position, close your eyes and tune into your body. Make sure your spine is lengthened so that the energy can flow freely. Scan your body for tension. Inhale and breathe into the area where it feels tight and then release the tension with your out-breath. Visualize the tension as a colour, and as you exhale, see that colour leaving your body. Once your body and mind are completely relaxed, ask yourself the following questions:

- What emotions am I feeling right now?
- What prompted these emotions? Was it a recent event or a past memory that has resurfaced?
- Where do I feel these emotions in my body?
- On a scale of 0 to 10, how intense do these emotions feel right now?

It's okay if you don't have clear answers. Let the process unfold naturally.

If your emotions feel intense, know that you don't need to force anything. The goal is not to fix or suppress, but to create space for feeling, space for grounding, space for softening. Next, start tapping on these feelings. It is okay if you don't want to name the emotions, you can simply tap on 'these emotions'.

Start with the set-up statement whilst tapping on karate chop point:

- *Even though I'm feeling a lot right now, I choose to be kind and gentle with myself.*
- *Even though this feels overwhelming, I honour what I'm feeling and allow myself to take this moment slowly.*

- *Even though there's so much coming up, I choose to create a safe space within me to just be with what is here.*

Round 1

Top of the head:
There's a lot moving through me right now.
Eyebrow:
I feel these emotions rising.
Side of the eye:
It feels like too much, and that's okay.
Under the eye:
I am safe to feel what I feel, at my own pace.
Under the nose:
I don't need to fix anything right now.
Chin point:
I don't need all the answers right now.
Collarbone:
Just noticing what's here.
Under the arm:
Breathing into this feeling.

Round 2

Top of the head:
I'm not alone. I'm here for myself.
Eyebrow:
I allow myself to feel, gently and safely.
Side of the eye:
Maybe I don't have to figure it all out right now.
Under the eye:
It's okay to pause and just breathe.
Under the nose:
I don't have to stay strong all the time.

Chin point:

These emotions are part of my healing.

Collarbone:

I give myself permission to take this one breath at a time.

Under the arm:

I honour the strength it takes to feel.

Round 3

Top of the head:

I am not defined by my past.

Eyebrow:

I am not defined by my emotions.

Side of the eye:

I'm choosing to simply be.

Under the eye:

I am safe. I am supported.

Under the nose:

Coming back to the centre.

Chin point:

And trusting that everything will work out just fine.

Collarbone:

This too shall pass.

Under the arm:

I am safe.

Tap on heart space (thymus):

Releasing these emotions in my mind and body so I can completely relax. All is well. I am safe.

Continue to tap on this until you feel completely relaxed and then place your hands on your chest and seal in the energy. As you breathe out, let go of any lingering emotions, and then check in with your body and rate the emotional intensity again. If there's still something there, you can repeat the tapping until the intensity goes down all the way to zero if that feels right for you. The goal isn't to rush or force it, but to find calm and clarity in your own time. Once there's no intensity left, anchor the energy by saying, 'Transform.'

Mind mapping your progress

I discovered the mind mapping technique a long time ago while studying architecture at university. It is a simple yet powerful tool for exploring ideas by laying out everything that is on your mind and translating it into a spider diagram for analysis and development. The beauty of a mind map is that you can jot down your thoughts freely and then create links between them. We can use the same technique to organize our thoughts and gain insight into our behavioural patterns and opportunities for improvement. A mind map can help you dissect and organize your thoughts in a logical way so you can gain clarity and an overview of a situation.

In the 2002 film *Minority Report*, John Anderton, played by Tom Cruise, stands in front of an interactive screen, reviewing evidence of a crime that is yet to be committed. He grabs and moves images around as he pieces together the sequence of events and tries to make sense of the bigger picture. Perhaps technology will one day allow us to do this in the privacy of our homes, but for now, the good news is we can gain a similar overview using the mind mapping technique.

Mind mapping is a great tool for people who struggle with expressing themselves through writing. It also takes less time than journalling. Reflection doesn't always have to be written in full sentences; it can be creative too. You can use words, doodles, and even colours to help you process what you're feeling or working through. The main objective of this exercise is to transfer everything that is taking up space in your head onto paper so you can get a bird's-eye view of it all.

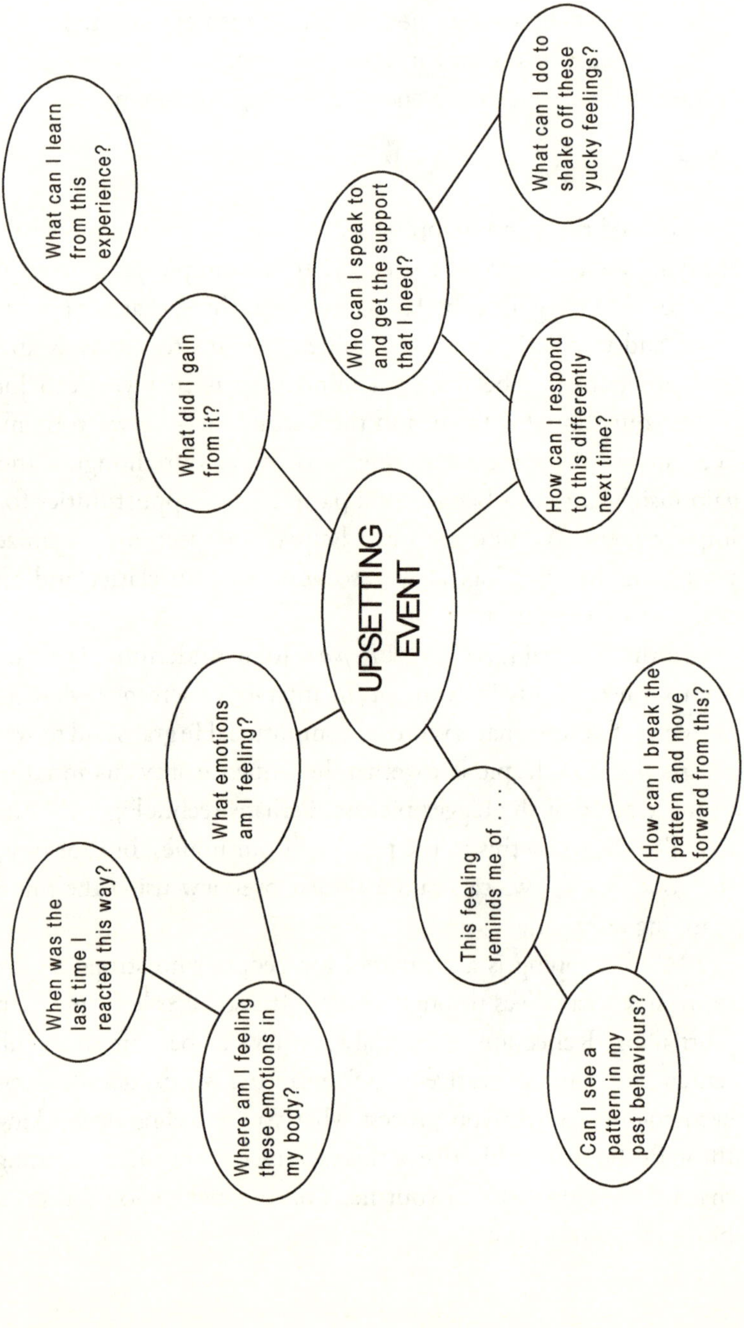
UPSETTING EVENT
What did I gain from it?
What can I learn from this experience?
Who can I speak to and get the support that I need?
What can I do to shake off these yucky feelings?
How can I respond to this differently next time?
What emotions am I feeling?
Where am I feeling these emotions in my body?
When was the last time I reacted this way?
This feeling reminds me of . . .
Can I see a pattern in my past behaviours?
How can I break the pattern and move forward from this?

Mind mapping is an effective way to declutter your mind, free up mental space and create room for insight and solutions.

Forgiveness meditation and tapping script

Here are two practices I like to use for forgiveness. Just like any therapeutic exercises in this book, it is important to seek support if you are processing a major traumatic event. Forgiveness is not a substitute for therapy, and you don't have to do it alone. If you've experienced serious harm or abuse, you are not being asked to take blame for what was done to you. This work is about releasing any internalized shame or guilt, not excusing those who caused harm. If forgiveness feels inaccessible right now, that's completely valid. For trauma or complex wounds, please consider working with a therapist or trauma specialist who can support your healing journey.

Step 1: Find a comfortable seated position, either in a chair or on the floor. Make sure your spine is straight, your head is neutral, and your shoulders are soft.

Step 2: Close your eyes and take a few deep breaths—in through the nose, out through the mouth. Allow your body to start letting go of tension.

Step 3: Ground yourself by feeling the weight of your body. If you are seated in a chair, notice the contact between your feet and the floor. Feel supported by the earth beneath you.

Step 4: Begin to focus on your breath. Notice the rise and fall of your body. Observe the breath entering your nose, filling your lungs, and leaving your body.

Step 5: Scan your body for any tension or discomfort. As you breathe in, gently bring awareness to the area. On the out-breath, imagine releasing that tension. You may choose to give it a colour and visualize it leaving your body.

Step 6: Once you get to complete stillness, bring to mind someone who has caused you pain, intentionally or unintentionally. Picture them at a safe distance. Notice what emotions arise. Allow yourself to acknowledge what you might want to say to this person. Keep this simple, you don't need to relive the entire story, just honour what's present.

Step 7: When you're ready, say silently to them: 'I forgive you for the ways you have hurt me. I forgive you.' Repeat this at your own pace. Focus on the feelings that surface and allow them to move through you, without getting lost in the story.

Step 8: Shift your focus now to yourself. Visualize a specific moment you want to forgive yourself for. Bring it into your awareness and say quietly: 'I forgive you.' Repeat until you feel the emotion begin to soften. There is no need to force anything, just stay with it until it feels like enough.

Step 9: Let go of the images or thoughts. Come back to your breath and your body. Gently place your hands over your heart, right hand on top of the left. Take a few more grounding breaths, giving thanks to yourself for showing up. When you are ready, open your eyes and return to the present.

Tapping script for forgiveness

Before we begin, take a deep breath. Ground yourself, then bring to mind someone you are struggling to forgive, or something you want to forgive yourself for. Rate the emotional intensity on a scale from 0 to 10.

Start tapping gently on the chop point for the set-up statement:

- *Even though I'm finding it difficult to forgive, I choose to love and accept myself.*

- *Even though there are people that I'm finding difficult to forgive, I choose to love and accept myself.*
- *Even though I'm finding it difficult to forgive myself, I choose to deeply love and accept myself anyway.*

Round 1

Top of the head:

This resistance.

Eyebrow:

All this resistance to forgiveness.

Side of the eye:

I find it so hard to forgive the people who have hurt me.

Under the eye:

I need to protect myself from getting hurt so I can't forgive them

Under the nose:

This resistance to forgiveness . . .

Chin point:

. . . feels like the only way I can protect myself.

Collarbone:

[Acknowledge the main reason for not forgiving yourself and others. For example, 'If I forgive, it feels like I'm saying what they did was okay,' or, 'If I forgive, it's likely they will do it again.']

Under the arm:

But what if forgiveness is actually the better way to protect myself?

Round 2

Top of the head:

What if forgiving them means I can finally free myself.

Eyebrow:

Wouldn't it be a relief to release this pain?

Side of the eye:

Wouldn't it be a relief to stop carrying this anger?

Under the eye:

I am open to the idea of forgiveness.

Under the nose:

Maybe I'm ready to release the burden.

Chin point:

It feels safer now to begin forgiving.

Collarbone:

I am learning to forgive myself for holding onto this pain.

Under the arm:

I'm ready to let go of the past.

Tap on heart space (thymus):

Releasing these emotions and allowing my body to relax.

Round 3

Top of the head:

Releasing the anger [or any emotion you are feeling] in my shoulders and chest [or any physical sensations you are feeling].

Eyebrow:

Letting go of the tightness in my heart.

Side of the eye:

I am ready to forgive.

Under the eye:

I am ready to be free.

Under the nose:

It's safe to let go now.

Chin point:

I am forgiving the people who hurt me, one breath at a time.

Collarbone:

I am forgiving myself for the pain I have carried.

Under the arm:

I am safe now.

Tap on heart space (thymus):

Breathing out all the tension . . . relaxing into this new space.

Place your hands on your chest and seal in the energy. Take a deep breath into your heart space, and as you exhale, release any tension you're still holding. Now gently check in and rate the emotional intensity again on a scale from 0 to 10.

After tapping, you may find the emotion has softened all the way to zero, or it might still be lingering, hovering around a two or higher. If it feels like something is stuck and won't shift, this could be a sign of what's known in EFT as psychological reversal (PR), a common block when dealing with strong or long-held emotions.

Psychological reversal (PR)

As mentioned earlier, anger and other emotions can sometimes prevent the emotional intensity from dropping, such as staying at a six even after a few rounds of tapping. This often points to an unconscious resistance to letting go. In EFT, we call this psychological reversal (PR). It happens when part of us, deep down, doesn't actually want to let go, most likely because holding on feels safer, or somehow necessary. It could be a need to hold someone accountable, or a belief that letting go would mean condoning what they did.

PR can block the effectiveness of tapping until it is addressed, which is why acknowledging and tapping on the resistance itself can be an important step in the healing process. This internal block can interfere with your ability to shift the energy, no matter how much tapping you do. So, when you feel stuck, try asking yourself:

- If there is a reason why I don't want to let go of this anger, what would it be?
- For example, 'He doesn't deserve to be forgiven after everything he did.'
- If there is a reason I want to keep holding onto this pain, what would it be?
- Such as, 'If I forgive her, she'll think what she did was okay.'

Once you have identified what is beneath the resistance, tap a few rounds on that specific belief or feeling. An exercise to demonstrate the same is mentioned below.

Tapping away resistance

Tap on the karate chop/ side of the hand point for set-up statement:

- *Even though part of me is still holding on, because I don't want to let them off the hook, I choose to honour how I feel and allow healing at my own pace.*
- *Even though I'm afraid letting go means it was okay, I acknowledge this fear and I choose peace.*
- *Even though part of me doesn't feel safe letting this go, I'm open to the possibility of release, one step at a time.*

Top of the head:

This remaining resistance.

Eyebrow:

Part of me is still holding on.

Side of the eye:

It feels safer to keep this anger.

Under the eye:

Maybe I'm not ready to forgive just yet.

Under the nose:

And that's okay.

Chin point:

I honour the part of me that's been protecting me.

Collarbone:

It's done its job well.

Under the arm:

But maybe it is safe to soften now.

Tap on heart space (thymus):

Letting go, only when I'm ready. I am safe.

Once you have tapped on the resistance, check in with yourself and rate the intensity again on a scale from 0 to 10. If there is still something lingering, you can continue tapping with a phrase like: '*Even though I still feel some of this remaining (emotion), I choose to be gentle with myself and let it go at my own pace.*' Repeat this process until the intensity is zero or you find yourself in a calmer, more peaceful state. To conclude, place your hands on your heart space and say, 'Transform'.

Cognitive reframing by tapping

Our emotions can affect us in numerous ways, especially our perception. When we are feeling optimistic, our perception of a situation tends to be more positive. This is why it is so important to use our emotions as a superpower to get ourselves unstuck. The way we see the world affects the narratives we create for ourselves. When we use healing to remove the emotional charge of past events, our thoughts and actions are no longer controlled by what happened in the past; this is when we can finally break free from repeated cycles.

In tapping, the change in perception is known as the 'cognitive shift'. When we reduce the emotional intensity while tapping on a specific past event, our perspectives can change as the emotions start to subside. We gain clarity and understanding of the situation so that any lingering hurtful feelings attached to the experience can be released.

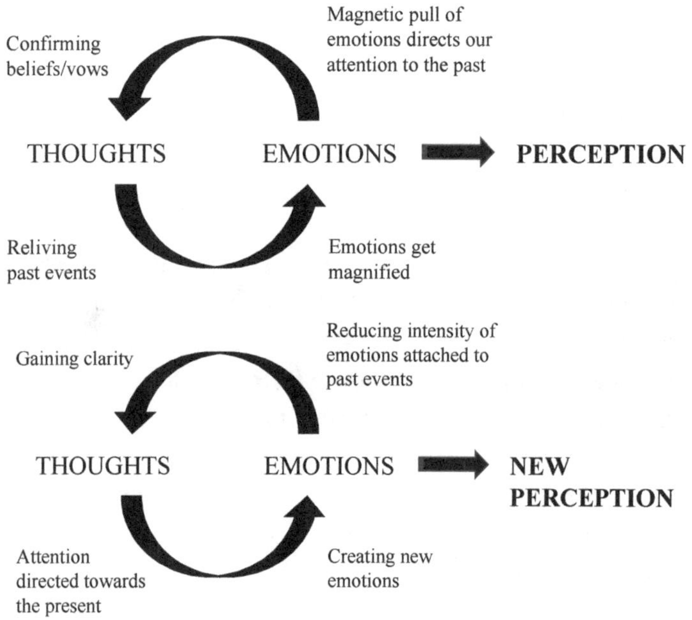

Figure 7.7: Forming perceptions

Emotions, when used wisely, are a powerful tool for navigating through life. By using emotions as a guide, we can trace back to the origins of the issue, remove the emotional charge, and reframe the memory of the event. How we frame a memory is more important than the memory itself. A traumatic event can have less of an impact on us when we can reinterpret it with greater understanding and acceptance. When a past event is only a memory, with very little or no emotional charge, we minimize the likelihood of blind reactions, such as saying things we don't mean when we get triggered. When we no longer react to the emotional triggers, there is less of a magnetic pull to take our attention away from the present and into the past. It becomes more effortless to stay present where all our attention is. Our past no longer dictates our present and future. We become unstuck.

Your Emotions Are Your Superpower

When we master our emotions by understanding them through observation and healing, we can use them as a superpower for navigating the ebbs and flows of life. We aim to respond rather than react, while allowing emotions to come through naturally. Let's say a friend says something offensive to you, and an unhealed wound of 'I'm not good enough' gets triggered, causing you to react with anger. Since energy is contagious, your friend also sees red and becomes defensive, accusing you of being too sensitive, which is probably triggered by her own past experiences. This battle can go on forever, with two people reacting to one another due to their own emotional triggers. It is fair to say that many arguments and misunderstandings can be avoided by doing inner healing work so we don't get offended so easily.

Emotional triggers can show us what needs to be healed, released, and made peace with. Being able to use your emotions to guide you through life is a self-mastery skill, and we all possess this superpower.

Healing Is Not Linear

I was once asked by a client, 'When am I going to be completely healed?' When we embark on a healing journey, we must bear in mind that healing is not linear; it doesn't have start and finish points. Healing is, in fact, an ongoing process of shedding years of conditioning and coming home to your true, authentic self. It is about recovering and reconnecting with your innate, pure, and joyful state of being. It is a journey that breaks you down and unravels all the bullshit you have been fed and the false identity you have created along the way. It is about undoing all your false beliefs about yourself so that you can love and accept yourself completely.

So, does healing have a finish line? No. It is a lifelong commitment. It is a process of acknowledging what we may need to heal from during the ups and downs of life. Change happens when we are going through difficult times. Healing takes place when we are in life's troughs, and it is okay to be there as long as we know how to bounce back. It is often in the darkness that we encounter opportunities to go within and heal, and then slowly but surely, we rise back up to the centre and reach the peak of a cycle again.

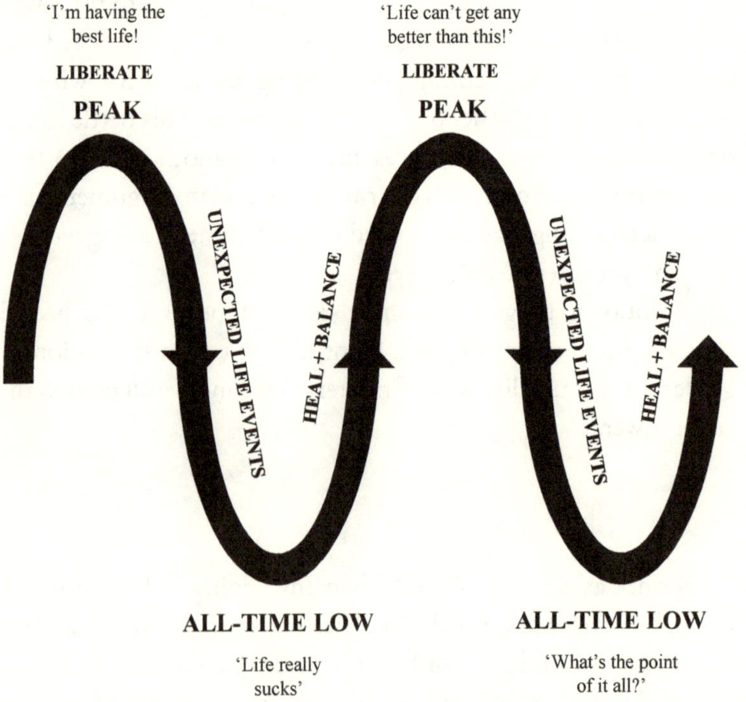

Figure 7.8: Bounce back by healing and balancing

Nature's cycles remind us that change is inevitable. Periods of change are often filled with pain and crisis, but in each period, there is potential for growth and self-mastery. No matter how much healing work we do, we cannot avoid the cyclical nature of life. However, we can change how we respond to it. Embracing change allows us to thrive. When we surrender to change rather than resisting it, we immediately snap out of survival mode and come back into the creative mode, the only place where growth can take place. When we know how to bounce back, falling into a low brings lessons we can learn from and shows us how we can better ourselves as we rise to the peak.

Healing is the catalyst for positive change within us. Eastern philosophies, including Zen Buddhism and Taoism, teach that balance arises from the interplay of yin and yang. To pursue balance, we must experience both highs and lows. Furthermore, contrast helps us appreciate the good things in life, the things for which we are grateful. If you never experience loss, you will never appreciate what you have gained. When life is all rainbows and unicorns, we lose the perspective that fuels growth and gratitude. Contrasts offer different perspectives and help us find direction and meaning in our journey. By embracing rather than resisting contrast, we align with nature's cyclical rhythm.

Just like the changing seasons, each life phase can reveal beauty and purpose that make life meaningful. Healing often takes root in our darkest moments. When we embrace these times as opportunities for growth, we soon find the light at the end of the tunnel and enjoy the fruits of our labour.

Let's look at the next stage of the UNSTUCK framework—balance.

8

Balance

'Tune in to find inner peace;
Declutter to prioritize what matters;
Recharge to gain momentum.'

—Mae Kwan

Coming Back to the Centre

There's a stage in the healing journey where it feels like a veil has been lifted. Suddenly, things become clearer. You begin to see yourself and life in a different light. There is a quiet shift in how you relate to the world around you. It might feel like a subtle settling inside, or it may be so profound that others begin to notice something different about you.

This is the moment you start reconnecting with your inner self. You begin to feel lighter as you let go of the beliefs, behaviours, and emotional burdens that no longer serve you. But you're not quite there yet. This isn't the finish line; it's the bridge. The next step is learning how to anchor that new awareness and stabilise the energy of the 'new you'.

For years, and sometimes, for decades, you have repeatedly processed the same thoughts, emotions, and reactions. Even after meaningful healing, it doesn't take much to fall back into old patterns. This is where balance begins: in that delicate space between insight and embodiment.

The tipping point

Time and again, I see my clients wanting change. In fact, they are desperate for change, but as soon as they reach the tipping point, fear starts to sneak in, and they fall back into their old habits and patterns. The fear of the unknown and the need to feel safe are the key factors that keep us in our comfort zone, no matter how loudly our inner voice is telling us to break free. Our self-limiting beliefs are so deeply ingrained that we choose to believe we need something outside of ourselves to change how we feel on the inside. In doing this, we give up our ability to make a change and break free from feeling stuck.

Take my client Sarah, for example. She was thinking about leaving a job that no longer fulfilled her. Deep down, she knew that staying meant remaining stuck and watching her potential go to waste. She took a brave first step and voiced her concerns to her seniors. Their response? A vague promise that if she kept showing dedication, she would be considered for promotion someday. It didn't shift how Sarah felt.

She found herself caught between staying and going, which kept her at the tipping point. There is no right or wrong in situations like these. The key is to make a decision, commit to it, and move forward in alignment with the outcome you want.

But Sarah didn't. She stayed in that stuck space for nearly a year, going back and forth in her head multiple times a day. This is what it looks like when we are stuck at the tipping point. Even when we are ready for change, old beliefs start to creep in:

- *What if I mess up?*
- *Isn't it safer to stay where I am? What if I can't find a job that's better than this one?*

- *What if the reason I still haven't been promoted is that I'm really not very good at what I do?*
- *I can't afford to leave this job.*

Figure 8.1: The tipping point

Sound familiar? This is the internal dialogue we have when we can't make up our minds. The lack of self-belief and the fear of uncertainty keep us living in the status quo. If you want to get unstuck, you must recognize and become aware of this negative self-talk, especially when you are at the tipping point.

The truth is that instability and discomfort are part of the process. Change is a redirection, not a punishment. Discomfort doesn't mean you are on the wrong path; it just means you are stepping into something new. To shift our comfort zone, we have to stretch it. Each time we do that, we give ourselves the chance to grow.

When we move beyond our old narratives, we must accept and embrace the changes that come with a new story. Letting go of the need for control and allowing life to unfold naturally helps us see the bigger picture. In my experience, as I started to release old attachments and respond differently, a series of changes followed, each bringing me closer to the life I truly wanted. Every step we take triggers a chain of events that reinforces our choices. My advice is: buckle up, expect the unexpected, and enjoy the ride.

Stages of a Relapse

Relapse doesn't always look dramatic. It can be so subtle that we don't even notice it until we are right back where we started. Here is how I often see it unfold:

Stage 1: You step into the unknown, outside your comfort zone.

Stage 2: Fear starts to kick in when you don't feel you are in control; the future feels unpredictable, as you are no longer repeating old patterns.

Stage 3: You crave control when discomfort sets in.

Stage 4: Stress and anxiety arise as you realise how much you can't control.

Stage 5: You feel a strong urge to cope, fix, and manage.

Stage 6: You experience more agitation when unexpected challenges show up.

Stage 7: You feel increasingly out of control.

Stage 8: Your nervous system goes into survival mode due to the fear of the unknown and the lack of control.

Stage 9: You reach breaking point. '*I can't do this. It's too hard.*'

Stage 10: You retreat to what is familiar for a sense of safety and security, even if it keeps you stuck.

Based on my experience, it only takes one small incident or emotional trigger for us to revert to our old behaviours. The emergency switch is activated, and we automatically fall back into survival mode. But here's the good news: you are not the same person you once were. With self-awareness, you can recognise these moments sooner. You can correct your thoughts before being pulled into the rabbit hole of self-sabotage and feeling stuck.

Automatic reaction (gets stronger each time it gets repeated) → **Becomes a habit** → **Repeated pattern**

Awareness (the observer) → **Metabolization** → **New pattern**

Identifying old patterns early enough to make the necessary adjustments is key to prevention. I like to refer to this as the 'snap-out-of-it' method. When you notice a reaction beginning to surface, take a moment to pause and redirect your attention. This helps to interrupt the automatic cycle of reactivity. Awareness allows us to acknowledge our emotions and enables them to flow through us. By honouring our feelings, we recognize that our body is responding to past hurts that are being triggered, giving them the space they need to be processed. With repeated practice, this new response will gradually become your default setting. The more aware you become of your emotions, thoughts, and behaviours, the more control you have to shift your mindset. As you raise your self-awareness and engage in healing work, your brain will adapt to this new way of thinking, making it easier to maintain balance over time.

Helpful Reaction Vs Unhelpful Reaction

Let's discuss the limbic brain and why it is essential to have automatic reactions despite the unpredictable nature of this in-built survival instinct. When faced with a threat, our survival instinct allows us to react quickly without the need to analyse the situation. For instance, if you are crossing the road and suddenly hear a car honk, your body instinctively jumps back to safety. This automatic response is crucial in protecting us from harm.

However, living in a constant fight-or-flight mode and interpreting every inconvenience as a threat can lead to unhelpful reactions, such as getting stressed in traffic or feeling frustrated when someone cuts in line. The goal is to preserve the survival instinct for real danger while doing the inner work needed to avoid living in a constant state of fear. When we live in fear, we experience emotional overwhelm, and our bodies remain on high alert. This prevents vital functions like digestion, regulation, and repair from operating efficiently. This is why emotional regulation is so important; it allows us to function at an optimal level.

Emotional Regulation for Balance

When we are under chronic stress, even the smallest irritations can trigger strong emotional responses. These reactions are often linked to unresolved past experiences. Our limbic brain responds to perceived threats faster than our logical brain can catch up, especially when we are already in a heightened state of fight or flight. In these moments, it becomes harder to regulate our emotions.

An automatic reaction is a deeply embedded defence mechanism. It kicks in when we feel emotionally threatened, such as when someone challenges or criticises us. One common trigger in heated conversations is the need to be right, which often arises when we feel unheard or that our opinions are undervalued. This response usually stems from a sense of inadequacy, hindering productive discussions where both viewpoints can be considered. Such reactivity causes us to lose sight of logic when we perceive a situation as a potential threat.

As explained previously, the limbic brain takes over when it detects an emergency and reacts on impulses. To become less reactive, we must investigate why we get triggered so easily in the first place. Emotional regulation requires us to identify the root cause of what is causing the discomfort and prompting us to defend ourselves. EFT tapping is a useful tool for using our emotions to guide us to the past events that may have caused this sense of insecurity. When we become more self-aware and listen to our emotional cues, we gain the ability to neutralize the emotional intensity, leading us to become less reactive as a result.

Understanding why we often find ourselves in a defensive or reactive state can become clearer with reflection, however, practising this awareness requires time and patience. The more we practise, the easier it becomes to differentiate between real danger and perceived threats. To restore balance while becoming less reactive, we can use the following quick-fix tool for emotional regulation.

A simple breathwork exercise for emotional regulation

When a strong emotion arises and the urge to react kicks in, the first step is to pause. Begin by taking a normal inhalation through your nose and then slowly release the breath through your mouth while dropping your shoulders and closing your eyes. Make sure that the out-breath is longer than the in-breath (for example, breathe in for four seconds and breathe out for eight seconds). Keep your eyes closed and allow yourself to sit with the emotion until it subsides.

The key component of this exercise is self-awareness. By becoming fully aware of our thoughts and emotions, we can take appropriate actions to bring ourselves back into balance. One simple way to do this is through conscious breathing. When we exhale for longer than we inhale, it helps calm the nervous system by activating the parasympathetic response, bringing the body and mind into a more relaxed state.

In a work situation, we can request a time-out by saying, 'Please give me a moment,' while subtly taking a long, slow exhale. This gives us a chance to self-regulate and release the tension that's building up in our system, without needing to explain or justify ourselves.

The Pendulum Effect

The healing journey is an ongoing process. Just when we think we have moved past something, old patterns or new coping mechanisms can resurface. This phenomenon is what I refer to as the 'pendulum effect'. Setbacks can be discouraging, and it is disheartening to feel motivated after a breakthrough, only to experience a regression. Emotional setbacks can be exhausting and confusing. At this tipping point, we often feel out of balance as our emotions fluctuate between feeling liberated and defeated. When our old beliefs resurface and we encounter roadblocks, we may find ourselves asking, 'When is this going to end? Why is this still happening to me? What more can I do?'

This is not the time to criticize yourself or think that making progress is impossible. You might be surprised to know that the opposite is true. If you are experiencing the pendulum effect, it means you have put in the work to reach this point. The next step is to anchor this new energy by making the necessary adjustments to return to a balanced state, rather than swinging from one extreme to another.

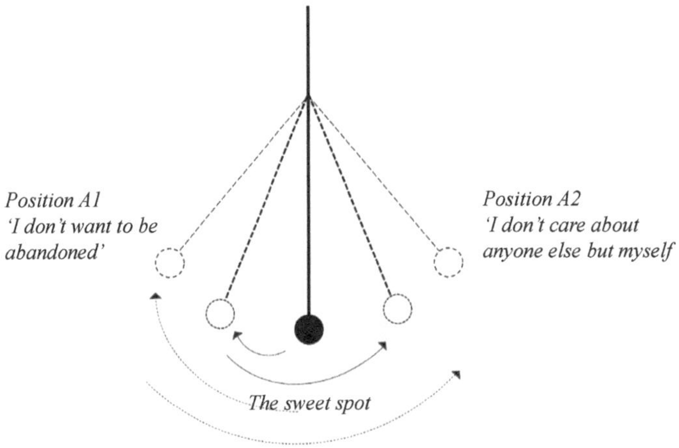

Figure 8.2: The pendulum effect

In the UNSTUCK framework, we not only use our emotions to rewrite the narrative, but we also focus on maintaining equilibrium in our new reality. Resilience is what helps us stay centred when things get tough. Let's take a closer look at the pendulum metaphor.

In figure 8.2, position A1 of the pendulum represents one end of the spectrum. In this position, the negative force is created by a fear of abandonment stemming from past experiences. The pain is intense, and this fear is deeply ingrained in your mind. When you attempt to overcome the belief that led to this fear, the intensity of your emotions can swing the pendulum to position A2 at the opposite end, often by frustration and anger. Here, you may adopt the belief 'I don't care about anyone else but myself'. This belief is also driven by the fear of abandonment, even though position A2 may feel like empowerment. In position A2, you do everything you can to avoid being abandoned, but you are also closing yourself off from the possibility of future connections.

Both positions are fuelled by fear and a need to protect ourselves from emotional pain and disappointment.

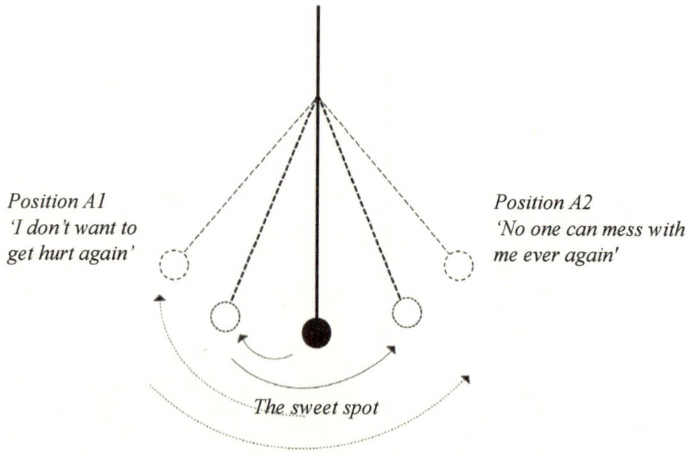

Figure 8.3: The pendulum effect

Consider the example of the grieving process following a loss. The pendulum effect can occur when we are processing deep and heavy emotions, especially when the fear of abandonment or rejection runs deep. In figure 8.3, position A1 of the pendulum represents the extreme end of the spectrum, where the belief 'I don't want to get hurt again' takes hold.

This negative force is created by feeling unsafe as a result of past experiences. During the process of getting unstuck, the emotional momentum may swing us to the other extreme, towards the belief, 'No one can mess with me ever again.' This position often creates a mirage of inner strength that can take a considerable amount of time for us to acknowledge. As mentioned previously, even though position A2 feels like a new, stronger version of you, it is still anchored in fear and self-protection. Sadly, it often leads to more suffering, as life is viewed through a fearful lens.

One way to soften the pendulum swing is to bring in love to help us feel safe enough to stop being on guard. When we feel safe, we don't need to protect ourselves so tightly. A simple act, such as placing a hand on the heart and practising the phrase 'I am safe' can remind the body that it's okay to settle. Other small ways to reconnect with that sense of safety include taking slow, deep breaths, feeling your feet firmly on the ground, or wrapping yourself in something comforting. Gentle yoga poses, like child's pose (*balasana*) or corpse pose (*savasana*), can also help by encouraging surrender and deep relaxation, offering the body a chance to rest and feel supported. These simple acts send signals to the nervous system that it's safe to let go, allowing the tension to ease and the pendulum to begin returning to centre, where balance lies.

The pendulum effect can show up throughout our lives whenever we don't feel 'safe'. The key is developing enough awareness to recognize this shift and knowing how to bring yourself back to centre. It only takes one triggering event to push you off balance, which is why regular self-check-ins and small course corrections are so important.

Finding the 'sweet spot' and maintaining our inner rhythm

Adversity can bring up memories of past failures, triggering emotions and limiting beliefs that make it difficult to manage stress. When will this end? Will I ever find a way out of this situation? It often feels like life keeps throwing unexpected challenges our way, no matter how hard we try to push through. In our fast-paced lives, we can easily feel scattered and swept away by the ups and downs. Therefore, we must establish a steady internal rhythm by continually returning to our 'sweet spot'. Bruce Lee's analogy of embodying the nature of water perfectly illustrates how we can navigate life's uncertainties.

> Be like water making its way through cracks. Do not be assertive, but adjust to the object, and you shall find a way around or through it. If nothing within you stays rigid, outward things will disclose

> themselves. Empty your mind, be formless. Shapeless, like water. If you put water into a cup, it becomes the cup. You put water into a bottle and it becomes the bottle. You put it in a teapot, it becomes the teapot. Now, water can flow or it can crash. Be water, my friend.[26]

When we release control, we remove the resistance that keeps us from adapting. The more adaptable we are, the more resilient we become in the face of adversity.

When you find yourself experiencing a setback or a bad day, just take it easy and use mindful practices to bring peace to the internal chaos and find strength in the stillness and joy of being alive. We are not meant to charge forward all the time; it is just as important to pause and reflect. It's okay not to make any progress. It's okay to take one step forward and two steps back. You just need to regain momentum by resetting and recharging. Balance is knowing how to come back to the 'sweet spot' every single time.

Allowing yourself to sit with the fluctuations and showing yourself compassion for how far you have come naturally neutralizes the charge. The more you resist, the harder the pendulum swings back. The trick is to be still. Yes, you read that right; the key to staying in balance is to do nothing but be still. By carving out time each day to quiet the mind, we create the inner stability needed to move through life with more ease. In doing so, we become more resilient, more centred, and more capable of handling whatever comes our way.

Another approach I often use is evaluating and anchoring my inner rhythm. With all the noise and chaos around us, cultivating self-awareness to stay grounded is essential. In today's world of instant gratification and constant stimulation, we are easily swept up in the chase for the next achievement or dopamine hit. Rather than savouring what's already here, we remain in pursuit

---

26 Bruce Lee and John Little, dir., *Bruce Lee: A Warrior's Journey*, Warner Home Video, 2000.

of what's next, missing the beauty and connection available in the present moment.

When we take time to tune into our inner rhythm, something shifts. We start noticing those subtle signals when we have drifted away from our natural flow—those times when we are pushing too hard or getting lost in the hypnotic pull of social media instead of listening to our inner wisdom. Meditation and mindful practices allow us to slow down and reconnect with our inner rhythm. In the space of stillness, we can differentiate between the frantic pace of the world and our natural cadence. These practices are not about achieving another goal; instead, they invite us to come home to ourselves and remember the wisdom that can only be found in stillness.

Changing Beliefs

The realization that our identities are shaped by external circumstances and the influence of others has been a transformative moment in my healing journey. We form beliefs about various aspects of our lives—our families, friends, colleagues, authorities, and the societies we live in. These beliefs shape our worldview and the roles we assume within it. Since childhood, our experiences have reinforced these beliefs, making it challenging to let go of the conditioned identities we have come to accept as truth.

The subconscious mind acts as a servant to the conscious mind during the imprinting process. The conscious mind is the logical part of our thinking; it learns new skills, processes information, and makes rational decisions. As we repeatedly engage in specific tasks and experiences, these actions become imprinted in our subconscious mind, transforming into autopilot behaviours. In order to change a belief, we have to reprogramme the subconscious mind so that we can change the ways in which we operate.

When we hold self-limiting beliefs, we often overlook opportunities or dismiss them outright because we don't believe we can achieve them. This choice is largely rooted in fear. As a result, we play it safe and unconsciously accept false beliefs such as 'I'm not good enough', 'I don't deserve love', or 'I'm unlucky'. However, when we shift our mindset and consciously alter these limiting beliefs into empowering ones, our entire perspective changes. We begin making decisions based on what our hearts truly desire. The more we repeat this new mindset, the more it becomes our default setting, allowing us to rewrite our internal programming.

Changing a belief requires you to make decisions based on new beliefs and then repeat them until they become the norm. The key is to identify which beliefs no longer serve us and what new beliefs we wish to adopt. Familiarity can create a false sense of security, making us cling to old thoughts and behaviours from the past, even when there is a strong desire for change. Making small adjustments is essential for establishing realistic momentum towards a new way of living. Although this may feel uncomfortable initially, with time and repetition, we can shift our paradigm by reinforcing new thoughts and inner dialogues in our subconscious mind. Repetition trains our minds, and over time, our brains will begin to change their neural pathways as new habits replace old ones.

As discussed by Dr Bruce H. Lipton, much of our day-to-day functioning operates on autopilot, driven by subconscious patterns.[27] The key is to rewrite these programmes that the subconscious mind operates on so that we can reshape our narrative, allowing for growth. Tapping can be a helpful tool for working with limiting beliefs, negative emotions, and negative self-talk, while introducing affirmations that help us focus on the positives. Regular tapping as

27 Bruce H. Lipton, '95 % Of The Day, You Are Not Operating From The Conscious Mind - Bruce Lipton,' posted August 26, 2021 by Success Archive, YouTube, https://www.youtube.com/watch?v=ZjZvtrKNvzU

a mindful practice enables us to recalibrate our thinking patterns towards more positive perspectives in any given situation.

Navigating Through the Void

When the world that feels like your reality is about to come to an end, a wave of discomfort and confusion usually surges in. I call this transition period the 'void'. The void is the grey area between the old and the new, the known and the unknown, the predictable and the unpredictable. This stage can feel extremely uneasy and, at times, disturbing, as the mind craves familiar and predictable outcomes. When you are in the void, you can feel extra sensitive to external stimuli, such as unexpected challenges and uncertainty, since nothing is yet set in stone.

We can think of this in-between stage as being like the healing of a physical wound. When we get a cut or scrape, the body's response system takes care of the injury by stopping the blood flow, fighting inflammation, and repairing the damaged tissue. Once the body starts to rebuild new skin, the injured area can feel raw and sensitive before the skin gets strengthened. Being in the void is like having this new skin that hasn't quite normalized. It feels weird to touch, and it can get a bit itchy, irritated, and uncomfortable.

This part of the get-unstuck process can invoke the fear of the unknown. The discomfort can be so unbearable that you want to give up and return to the old way of living, which feels much easier than venturing into the unknown, where nothing is guaranteed. This stage is necessary, despite its awkwardness, because healing creates change. We simply cannot get unstuck while staying the same. Things have to get shaken up and broken down so we can rebuild a stronger and better foundation. We resist change because it represents something different, something risky, and something that doesn't guarantee safety. Change creates discomfort because our internal system is always seeking what we already know, which provides safety and security.

However, when we allow ourselves to sit patiently in the discomfort and let our systems get used to new routines and patterns, we begin to stabilize the transformation and step into the next chapter with more clarity and confidence.

This is also the point where we start embodying a new version of ourselves. Instead of focusing solely on what needs to be changed or fixed, it is far more effective to shift our attention to the person we are becoming. When we stay connected to why we wanted to get unstuck in the first place and hold a clear vision of the version of ourselves we are stepping into, it becomes easier to make aligned decisions, even when the discomfort is still present.

In *Atomic Habits*, James Clear explains that the most effective way to create lasting change is to build identity-based habits[28] Rather than focusing on outcomes or behaviour alone, we begin by shifting our identity. For example, instead of saying, 'I need to stop people-pleasing,' which still keeps our focus on the unwanted habit, we can begin to affirm: 'I'm someone who honours my own needs.' This subtle shift reinforces the new way of being. We are not just trying to change what we do; we are committing to who we are becoming. When that identity becomes something we believe in, even just a little, our actions begin to reflect it more naturally.

Habitual patterns can be incredibly difficult to break, especially when they have formed around fear, survival, or the comfort of what once felt familiar. This was true in my own experience. It is tempting to go back to what we know, even if it doesn't serve us any more, because there's safety in familiarity. But this is exactly why it is essential to keep reconnecting with the deeper intention behind our healing. Why did I want to get unstuck? Who am I becoming through this process? These questions help to keep us grounded and committed to the path, even when it feels difficult.

---

[28] James Clear, *Atomic Habits: An Easy & Proven Way to Build Good Habits & Break Bad Ones* (Avery, 2018), chapter 2.

Breaking the Cycle with Self-Regulation

We know that avoiding pain and discomfort can cause stagnation in our journeys to get unstuck, but how do we break the cycle and create momentum again? Trust me, I have been there. The pain can feel so real that it seems easier to push uncomfortable thoughts and feelings out of our consciousness than to reflect on them. However, unpleasant emotions don't just disappear; they always find a way to show up again to get our attention. In my journey, I have learned to self-regulate my emotions through movement, breathwork, tapping, and meditation. These mindful practices are great quick-fix tools for emergency use, such as when an important meeting has gone horribly wrong, when you can feel rage bubbling up during a heated conversation, or when you feel frustrated with having to multitask house chores while managing a screaming child in the background.

We all have moments when we feel we are going to lose it. However, there is a lot of shame attached to the idea of an emotional breakdown, so we have learned to dismiss these emotions and suck it up rather than allowing them to move through us. Suck it up demands that we avoid feeling the emotions. It also means that we are judging the emotions that highlight unresolved aspects of our lives that need our attention. When we stop judging our negative emotions, we stop resisting the signals that are there to show us the internal imbalance.

While processing emotions is an important part of the get-unstuck journey, I'm not going to deny how easy it is to get pulled into a whirlwind of self-judgement and criticism. As well as taking quiet time to reflect and reset, another effective way to break the cycle is to engage in an activity that brings you joy. Find out what makes you feel good—is it exercise? Dancing to your favourite tune? Going for a long walk in nature? Here are some ways to break free from a negative thought loop. These mental and physical exercises are immediate stress relievers that can calm your body's stress response when you are feeling stressed and overwhelmed. They will help you become less reactive and more empowered to break out of the cycle.

Immediate stress relievers for breaking a negative cycle

- **Breathwork** uses conscious, controlled ways of breathing to influence our mental, emotional, and physical states. Conscious breathing techniques can help calm our minds and relax our bodies. Just taking a few deep inhales and exhales can bring us back to a calmer state. The following breathing exercise is great for reducing stress and anxiety by slowing your exhale through an imaginary straw.

Straw breathing

1. Find a comfortable sitting position.
2. Take a normal inhalation and then exhale and relax your whole body.
3. Do a few more rounds of mindful breathing. Connect with your body and make sure you are comfortable and relaxed.
4. Inhale normally and then exhale fully through an imaginary drinking straw.
5. Repeat this for three to five minutes or until you feel calm and peaceful.

- **Tapping** is a great way to calm the nervous system in moments of stress and anxiety. You may feel uncomfortable doing the complete tapping sequence in an emergency or in a public space, but you can simply breathe deeply, touch or tap on the corner of your thumbnail and fingersnails. Finger tapping can release the intensity of our emotions, making it a great self-soothing technique.

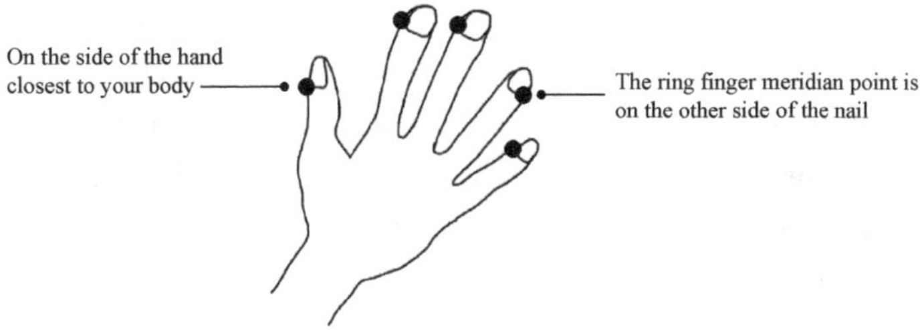

Figure 8.4: Finger tapping points

- Sports or any **physical activities** that you enjoy and that require your full attention, so your focus is on the present moment. My personal favourites are tennis and swimming.
    - Yoga is a mindful practice that works with the mind–body connection. It is important to focus on the breath during the practice. The synchronization between the breathing pattern and yoga movement can calm the mind and reduce stress levels.
    - A long walk in nature can help ground yourself. This exercise is best done alone. Notice everything that surrounds you to stay present.
    - Dance or any kind of fun, mindful movements.

The best type of quick-fix tool is something that you truly enjoy. This is pivotal to ensuring that our new belief system is firmly anchored when breaking a negative cycle. When we keep 'penduluming' between the old and new patterns, this can lead to fear-based stagnation or the possibility of relapse.

Be Fluid

Our need to feel safe often makes us cling to control, even when it holds us back. But true freedom comes when we stop trying to manage every outcome and start trusting the process instead. The more we loosen our grip, the more fluid we become. Letting go of control doesn't mean we stop caring, it means we make space for possibilities we can't always see when we are stuck in fear.

To flow around obstacles, we have to let go of expectations that can hinder our response to unforeseen challenges. Let's face it, we can never predict all the risks involved in any situation, so what is the point of stressing over them? If we master our emotions and respond to challenges by directing our focus towards finding solutions, there will always be a way out of any tricky situation.

It is important to be aware of the challenges ahead without fixating on them. Being aware means acknowledging their presence without denying them while consciously focusing on the actions needed to overcome those obstacles. When this happens, we stay in creative mode rather than slipping into survival mode. We respond rather than react. The key is to keep our awareness in the present while acknowledging what lies ahead. I admit this is probably the hardest thing to do when life becomes overwhelming. How do we redirect our thoughts when so many problems demand our attention? When we concentrate only on problems, particularly under pressure, it becomes challenging to manage stress and anxiety. Anxiety consumes a lot of mental energy, making it hard to focus, and we end up operating in survival mode, which only makes problem-solving more difficult.

When you feel overwhelmed, meditation and mindfulness can help bring clarity by quieting the mind. Our intuition emerges when the mind is still, so if we want to listen, we must embrace mindfulness as a daily practice. To remain fluid is to be still, for it is in stillness that we find the answers we seek.

Procrastination happens when we are fearful of making a move, taking action and making things happen. We come to a halt when fear kicks in. This fear is usually triggered by unexpected challenges and circumstances. This is the time to check in with yourself and observe the negative self-talk playing on repeat in your head. With awareness, you can spot this inner conflict that arises when you haven't quite anchored the new version of yourself. Part of you is determined to make changes towards a more fulfilling life, but another part is trying to talk you out of it.

Let's use the example of finding your dream job. Your dream is to work for a reputable advertising company. You took the first step by tidying up your CV and writing the perfect cover letter to showcase your talents and experience. You then took the next important step by contacting the top companies you want to work for. A couple of weeks go by, and you still haven't heard from any of them. You start to think perhaps you're dreaming too big and that these companies wouldn't consider you a suitable candidate, let alone offer you a chance to present your work face to face. You begin to lose hope, and fear starts to kick in. Perhaps you're just not good enough, or maybe luck is never on your side. Now that you've started doubting yourself, you begin to feel worried and agitated, but you still hope one of the companies will contact you out of the blue. You know you can't wait forever though, and over time, you decide to give up altogether and accept the belief that you are simply not good enough.

In this example, procrastination begins when you stop believing in yourself. Rather than actively exploring alternative options or following up on the emails you sent, you fall back into the old habit of negative thinking about your capabilities. Nothing positive comes from a negative mindset. When you read about successful people and their stories, you notice a major commonality: they never, ever give up.

Everyone experiences failure at some point; it is successful people's positive attitudes that get them unstuck and enable them to create success. Forward movement is crucial for avoiding stagnation, whether mental or physical. When you can't find a job, you can keep yourself active by enrolling in a course to upgrade your skills or volunteering as an intern to stay connected to your industry. There is a solution for every obstacle if we stay in creative mode by focusing on finding solutions, not dwelling on the obstacles themselves. When we choose to engage our minds in making things happen, we no longer waste energy on what causes stagnation and keeps us stuck.

UNSTUCK Toolbox for Balance

Setting the tone for the day

When you first wake up in the morning, do you feel the urge to check your smartphone for all the updates you missed while you were asleep? This can be one of the worst things you do for yourself at the start of the day. Upon waking, your brainwaves transition from delta (deep sleep) to theta (partially awake) and then to alpha (fully awake but relaxed). This alpha state can be disrupted as soon as you read or see something triggering, whether it's a work email reminding you of a looming deadline or distressing news from around the world. Within moments, stress-related thoughts can creep in, and your emotions may align with those thoughts even before you have gotten out of bed. How you feel throughout the day can be influenced by what you expose your mind to first thing in the morning. So, what's the best way to set a positive tone for the day?

- **Meditate**
  Meditation is one of the most effective ways to raise our awareness and prepare for the day ahead with a clear mind.

I like to think of it as 'cleaning house'. When we clear away the mental clutter, we can better tune into our intuition, where all the answers are available. This practice serves as an excellent detox for our mental well-being, especially when done consistently every day. Spending just five to ten minutes daily can leave you feeling lighter and more refreshed.

I recommend meditating first thing in the morning, but I'm not strict about it. Whenever I feel the need to declutter my mind, I make sure to set aside the time and space to tune in and reset.

- **Unplug**

  This is commonly referred to as a digital detox. Many of us rely on our phones for work, socializing, and planning, as they enable us to accomplish tasks efficiently. However, it becomes unhealthy when we find ourselves aimlessly scrolling through social media, watching endless YouTube videos, or frantically texting friends just to keep busy. I recognize that this can be a challenging issue; I often have to remind myself to stay in check. Each day, I consciously strive to ensure my mental state isn't hijacked or overstimulated by unnecessary distractions.

  Research has shown that excessive screen time can lead to distraction, increase stress, and negatively affect our sleep. If something consumes your thoughts and attention excessively, it can't be beneficial for you, right? By constantly checking emails, text messages, news updates, and social media to feel 'connected' to the digital world, you may actually be disconnecting from reality when your awareness shifts away from the present moment. I often notice people scrolling on their phones while walking down the street or during meals with friends and family. If this isn't an addiction, then I don't know what is.

Starting today, be mindful of how you use your devices and schedule regular breaks from screens throughout the day. Allow yourself the freedom to disconnect from the digital world so you can connect with yourself and your surroundings in the present moment. Don't give away your power by letting your phone take away your awareness. By consciously choosing when to engage with the digital world, we can become more attuned to what is happening within us and around us.

- **Organize personal space**
  My background in architecture, combined with my fascination with quantum physics, led me to study the principles of feng shui, which focus on balancing spatial energy flow and creating a harmonious living space. Having a sanctuary for daily rest and restorative rituals is essential for maintaining balance and anchoring our sense of self. The environments where we live and work significantly influence our mental well-being and reflect our personalities and inner states. For instance, someone with a messy room may feel overwhelmed and be more prone to anxiety and stress, suggesting a connection between our external environment and internal state. Sometimes chaos manifests outwardly, and sometimes our surroundings can create the chaos we feel.

  To fully benefit from feng shui principles in maintaining a harmonious life, it is important to remember that the space we create serves only as a container that complements the inner work we undertake. Progress can only be achieved by caring for our mental and physical well-being within the safe space we establish for ourselves. The energy flow in our outer environment and our inner selves go hand in hand. According to feng shui principles, stagnant energy, known as *chi*, in our living environment can hinder personal progress. By organizing and decluttering our homes and engaging in feng shui practices to balance the chi, we can create spaces that support and align with our inner state of being.

- **Release tension and regain balance in the physical body**
  Trauma expert and author of *The Body Keeps the Score*, Dr Bessel van der Kolk explains how trauma affects not only our minds but also our bodies.[29] He notes that the somatic memories of traumatic events and unresolved emotions can become trapped in our bodies, leading to chronic physical pain and illness if not addressed. Fortunately, there are various therapeutic methods available to release this stored trauma and emotion. These include tapping, somatic therapy, and mindful practices such as yoga.

  I am a huge fan of yoga. When it is practised mindfully, it creates a sense of calm, releases tension and discomfort in the body, and helps us become aware of any unresolved trauma that needs attention.

  Here are some of my favourite yoga poses:
  - Lotus pose for centring
  - Butterfly pose for opening the hips and aiding digestion
  - Forward bend for releasing tension in the lower part of the body
  - Plough pose for releasing tension in the neck and shoulders
  - Melting heart pose for releasing tension in the upper back
  - Spinal twist for releasing tension in the back

---

29 Bessel van der Kolk, 'What is trauma? The author of "The Body Keeps the Score" explains | Bessel van der Kolk | Big Think,' posted on September 17, 2021, by Big Think, YouTube, https://www.youtube.com/watch?v=BJfmfkDQb14

- Legs-up-the-wall pose for lowering stress and anxiety
- Happy baby pose for releasing hip and lower back tension
- Child's pose for recovery and grounding

• **Gratitude**

To maintain balance in our lives, we must cultivate a state of gratitude to avoid falling into a scarcity mindset, which focuses on what we lack. Embracing an abundance mindset, where we believe there is enough for everyone, allows us to be open to the greatness that can come our way. When we shift our perspective from scarcity to abundance, we create space for new opportunities to appear. With a more positive outlook, we find it easier to recognize these opportunities.

It can be extremely challenging to feel grateful when we're feeling stuck, particularly during negative spirals. Starting with small things can make a significant difference; a collection of little moments can generate a powerful sense of positivity and shift our energy. Daily gratitude practices, such as listing things for which we are thankful, can greatly improve our mood. It is important to appreciate both the simple pleasures and the significant events in life. Here are some gratitude practices to consider:

- **Journalling**
  You can write about a few people, things, and events that you feel grateful for every day.
- **Gratitude meditation**
  While falling asleep, mentally list the things you are thankful for. This exercise is a personal favourite of mine and can help ensure a restful night's sleep.
- **Gratitude jar**
  This is a great way to introduce gratitude exercises to kids at home. Place a jar on the breakfast table and

encourage each family member to write down a few things they are thankful for on a piece of paper. Fold the papers and place them in the jar. You can read these notes whenever you want to boost your mood or as part of a regular family bonding activity.

- **Celebrate your wins—big and small**

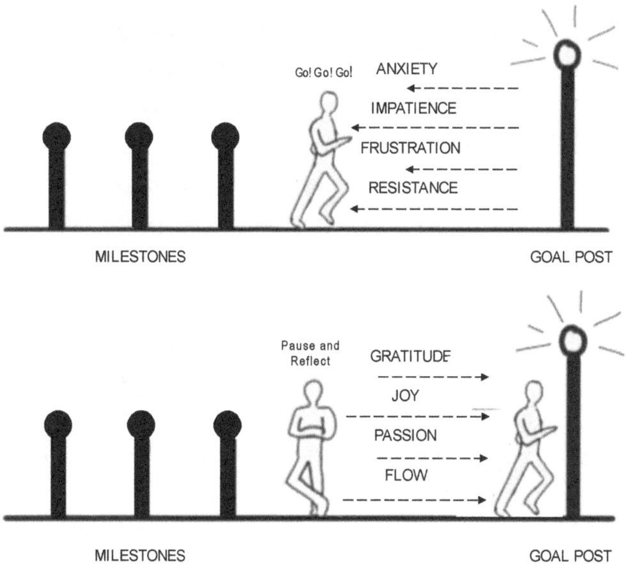

Figure 8.5: How to reach the goal post

We are taught to aim high from an early age, and while there is nothing wrong with having big dreams, we must recognise that change doesn't happen overnight. Achieving our goals involves a series of milestones, and focusing solely on the end goal can be disheartening. To maintain balance during this journey of getting unstuck, it is essential to celebrate small wins, take time to reflect on our accomplishments, and give ourselves a high five for staying on course. This practice helps keep us in a positive mindset, allowing us to continue moving in the right direction towards our desired experience.

Here are some ways to celebrate your wins:

The first step is to determine your 'wins'. Small wins can include completing a task, receiving a referral from a client, or starting a new training programme. Large wins might involve starting a new job, purchasing your first home, or securing a deal with a new client.

- Write down a list of goals you want to achieve on a monthly or quarterly basis. This milestone checklist provides a clear reference for both the small and big wins. When you achieve a win, take the time to celebrate it!
- Be creative with your celebrations. Do things you usually don't have time for, like gardening, hiking with your dog, or visiting a friend you haven't seen in a while.
- A celebration can be as simple as reflecting on your achievements and acknowledging how far you've come. Daily journalling is a powerful tool for cultivating gratitude and self-awareness.
- Create a wish list of celebrations. For small wins, consider treating yourself to a nice meal, and for bigger wins, think about a spa day or a golf trip.

- **Winding down**

  After a stressful day, it is vital to take time to relax and decompress; otherwise, our nervous systems may not have the opportunity to calm down properly. Practising relaxation techniques daily, especially at night, enables us to fully rest and recharge, leading to clearer thinking and better decision-making. With consistent practice, your body will adapt to this new habit, making it easier to unwind when it's time to rest. This, in turn, enhances your functioning the following day and promotes deeper sleep. While stress can be unavoidable and even necessary at times, it's important to prevent it from becoming chronic, as ongoing stress may lead to exhaustion, depletion, and ultimately, illness.

In addition to meditation, simply sitting quietly with your eyes closed for ten minutes can help both your body and mind relax. If you find sitting still challenging, consider lying down in Corpse Pose (Savasana) on a yoga mat as an alternative for this deep relaxation exercise.

Relaxing in Savasana pose

Step 1: Lie on your back with your legs extended and your feet hip-width apart, allowing them to drop slightly outwards to open the inner legs. If you feel discomfort in your lower back, you can bend your knees or rest your legs on a bolster to prevent your lower back from arching.

Step 2: Position your arms away from your body with your palms facing upwards.

Step 3: Begin a body scan to identify any areas of discomfort or tension. Start at your feet and move upwards through your legs, hips, abdomen, chest, back, and finally to the top of your head. Consciously release tension in each part by breathing deeply into that area, and as you exhale, imagine dissolving the tension. As you focus on your body and connect with your breath, allow yourself to turn inwards and check in with how you feel. Stay in this pose for as long as you need.

Step 4: To release the pose, gently roll onto your right side and pause briefly before moving back to a seated position.

- **Trust**

  When we feel lost and everything feels uncertain, this is when we must trust. Trust that we're not as far off course as we think, and that what's unclear right now may be guiding us somewhere we just can't see yet.

  Life is inherently unpredictable, whether it is your neighbour hosting a late-night party before your crucial meeting or your child falling ill as you prepare for a job interview. The only way to maintain a positive outlook is to trust that these unexpected events have a purpose. Challenges are presented to us as opportunities for growth and, most importantly, to guide us towards a better path if we acknowledge and understand the signs.

  Practices for building trust:

  - Tapping exercises can help reframe our thoughts when navigating adversity.
  - Mindful practices to quiet the mind and reduce negative self-talk can help bring us back to the centre and eliminate self-doubt.
  - A strong support network can keep you on track, providing the love and encouragement you need.

- **Find your tribe**

  The journey of self-discovery can often feel overwhelming and lonely. Having a strong support system and choosing the right people to be part of your tribe can make all the difference. Surround yourself with individuals who align with your outlook on life and will support your journey. I feel fortunate to have such a support network that has helped me through the process of getting unstuck. The connections I have inspire me to be the best version of myself, as I am loved and supported.

  Humans thrive on connection, and forming your tribe during your process of getting unstuck will enable your growth. These are the people who will support you during difficult times, cheer you on when you make progress, and encourage you to pursue your dreams. Ultimately, you want cheerleaders who will show up when you are feeling low and celebrate with you when you are on a high, rather than naysayers.

Your tribe should consist of people with whom you can have honest conversations. Frequently, people choose to be dishonest out of fear of discomfort rather than because they are incapable of telling the truth. They shy away from tough conversations and any kind of conflict. When you can't discuss issues honestly and resolve them openly, everything gets swept under the carpet. Gabor Maté explains, 'The person who does not feel or express negative emotion will be isolated even when surrounded by friends, because his real self is not seen. The sense of hopelessness follows from the chronic inability to be true to oneself on the deepest level. And hopelessness leads to helplessness, since nothing one can do is perceived as making any difference.'[30] When we don't feel safe enough to show up as our authentic selves, we still experience a sense of loneliness, regardless of how many friends we have or how busy our social calendar is. It's only when we connect with others on a deeper level, rather than a superficial one, that we can feel supported and not alone.

As Brené Brown states so eloquently in her book, *The Gifts of Imperfection*, 'Authenticity is a collection of choices that we have to make every day. It's about the choice to show up and be real. The choice to be honest. The choice to let our true selves be seen.'[31] Honesty is key to meaningful relationships; it enables you to connect with others at a much deeper level and form bonds that cannot easily be broken.

---

30 Maté, *When the Body Says No*, chapter 7.

31 Brené Brown, *The Gifts of Imperfection* (Simon and Schuster, 2022), eBook.

Bouncing Back from a Relapse

Setbacks are a part of life. During your transformation, you may occasionally fall back into old habits and behaviours. This is completely normal, and with awareness, you can either prevent these relapses or recognize them early enough to take steps to recover. In my coaching experience, I have observed that clients often shift from an empowering mindset to a disempowering one due to the fear of failure. Shame is often associated with the idea of failing, which can hinder our ability to bounce back after a relapse. The level of shame we associate with failure often stems from our upbringing. Traditional parenting sometimes relies on fear-based approaches to achieve desired outcomes, leading us to develop coping strategies to avoid failure later in life.

Another significant factor contributing to the fear of failure is imposter syndrome. This phenomenon is heavily influenced by our early experiences. For instance, individuals raised as the 'perfect child' may feel immense pressure to uphold that image, while those seen as the 'weaker sibling' might struggle with feelings of inadequacy. It is common for those dealing with imposter syndrome to constantly compare themselves to others, feeling like a fraud despite their accomplishments.

Feeling ashamed of failure can lead to stagnation, preventing us from taking risks. This can result in remaining stuck in an unhappy job or relationship, where familiarity provides a sense of stability and comfort, even if it is unfulfilling. Anything outside these familiar narratives represents unknown risks and discomfort. The fear of failure is triggered because humans tend to feel safest when things are predictable. This predictability creates a false sense of control, leading us to believe we have everything figured out when, in reality, we might just be ignoring or numbing our feelings of being stuck, too afraid to pursue a new path.

The truth is that no one can escape failure; even the most successful people have faced numerous setbacks. What sets them apart are their qualities of perception, resilience, focus, and determination, which help them stay on the path to success. They understand how to bounce back time after time. By shifting our perception from fearing failure to embracing it, we can uncover the valuable lessons that failures can teach us. Embracing failure and learning to bounce back are crucial for self-mastery.

Understanding the roots of our fear of failure, including the influence of our upbringing and experiences with imposter syndrome, can help us confront these fears more effectively and work towards personal growth and success. By recognizing that our fear often originates from childhood experiences or societal pressures, we can begin to challenge these ingrained beliefs and foster a healthier relationship with failure.

Failure is not the opposite of success; it is an essential part of the journey. We are all works in progress. Each setback and moment of uncertainty presents opportunities for growth and learning. By changing our perspective on failure, we can transform it from a source of fear and shame into a valuable resource for personal development and success.

Here are other methods you can use to bounce back from a relapse.

Flipping the switch

Unresolved emotions can feel intense due to the accumulation of emotional memories trapped within us. When we experience strong emotions triggered by a specific event, their intensity can feel electrifying and uncontrollable, making it difficult to detach from them. It is helpful to reframe our thoughts to defuse this emotional intensity and break free from the pull of our memories. By shifting our focus away from what is triggering us, the energy of these emotions begins to dissolve until it no longer has a hold on us.

Imagine being triggered by a comment from a friend about your appearance. Even if it wasn't their intention, you might perceive this remark as an attack, as it reminds you of a similar incident that caused you emotional pain. In this moment, your neural pathways may take you back to past thoughts and feelings, making you relive experiences that confirm your belief that you are not enough. Now, picture developing the ability to 'flip the switch' and transform this intense pain into something that serves you. Once you have flipped the switch and worked through the emotion, this energy can serve to move you forward instead of holding you back. You have the ability to make this shift, but you may wonder how to do it.

The following reframing exercise is one of the quick-fix tools discussed in my UNSTUCK workshop for recovering from negative thought-emotion cycles. You can use it whenever you find yourself spiralling into a victim mentality. Start reclaiming your power by tapping into the following statements:

- *I am comfortable in my own skin. I embody beauty inside and out.*
- *I accept all my emotions and let them move through me.*
- *I choose to trust myself to make the right decisions.*
- *I am open to the possibilities that life may bring in this new chapter.*
- *I am worthy of what I desire.*
- *I am courageous.*
- *I am fearless.*
- *I am enough.*

Continue tapping until you feel a shift within. Rate your experience and seal it. Remember that you have the power to detach from your emotional state and elevate your vibration to align with the new reality you wish to create. Turn your pain into power by flipping the switch and reframing your thoughts from negative to positive. Honour your feelings without judgement and choose to release them, making space for the new.

By expressing gratitude and acknowledging your worthiness, you release the need to be right, to seek validation, to pursue perfection, or to fill any perceived void within you. Recognize that your inner victim may rise when you get triggered, and view this as a cue for further healing. We are all works in progress, and experiencing setbacks is alright. When you stop striving for perfection, you can silence your inner critic and appreciate the journey of personal growth. Learning to be your own cheerleader makes it easier to maintain a positive mindset. There may be times when those around you don't believe in your potential, but don't let that discourage you from pursuing your goals.

Finding a new meaning

We can bring clarity to any situation by changing the way we perceive our experiences. Consider the example of injustice. When we feel wronged, a victim mindset encourages us to think, 'Poor me, sitting here suffering alone, when no one in this world can understand my pain.' This is a crucial moment when we need to recognise that such limiting thought patterns can isolate us, leading us to adopt the belief, 'It's me against the world.' To shift this mindset, we must look at the situation from a different perspective. Finding a new meaning can help us create a narrative that encourages growth.

Instead of allowing your inner peace to be dictated by external circumstances, use setbacks as an opportunity to make significant changes and necessary improvements. While we cannot control external events, we have complete control over our responses to them. Understanding this concept can help you navigate life's obstacles. We all face challenges, the only way forward is to confront them with an open mindset, viewing each hurdle as a redirection or an opportunity for something better. Trust that everything will eventually fall into place; nothing lasts forever. This too shall pass.

Staying active

Recent studies have shown that physical activities can activate our dopamine system and promote a more positive mindset. In addition to the long-term physical health benefits, staying active can help us snap out of a cycle of negative thought-emotion cycle by improving our emotional regulation abilities.

One habit I have incorporated into my routine for boosting my well-being is my weekly tennis training sessions. I grew up playing tennis regularly, but I stopped in my late teens because the pressure to perform well became too overwhelming. For many years, the fear of not being good enough kept me from returning to the sport. Fast forward twenty-six years, and I now play at least once a week simply because it brings me joy. Most importantly, I have developed a much more positive attitude towards tennis, which has allowed me to play better than ever. When you engage in an activity for your own happiness and satisfaction, you tend to excel. The joy of playing is what truly matters, not how well you play or what others think about your skills. Therefore, if you are feeling low and need a dopamine boost, consider taking up a sport that brings you joy and fulfilment.

Staying in Balance

How can we achieve emotional balance daily? Balance is not a constant state; it is unrealistic to expect to maintain eternal calmness and peace without putting in the necessary effort. Most of us have various roles to fulfil in both society and our personal lives. Typically, we find ourselves swinging between extremes, from chaos to calm, and sometimes drifting somewhere in between. It is important to remember not to judge yourself for occasionally feeling out of balance or lost. The key to maintaining balance is to recognize when you are not aligned and then take action to return to your centre.

Feeling balanced is a dynamic state; it is not static. We constantly sway between action and inaction, between being active and resting, and between high alertness and complete calm. The human body is perpetually seeking a state of homeostasis, or balance. The sympathetic and parasympathetic nervous systems work together to ensure that the body can carry out various internal activities, helping us regain balance. When we experience stress, the sympathetic response is activated, signalling the body to prepare for fight-or-flight mode by raising blood pressure, increasing heart rate, and slowing digestion. This survival response ensures our safety. Once the threat has passed, the parasympathetic nervous system takes over to restore the body to a state of homeostasis, lowering blood pressure, slowing the heart rate, and returning digestion to its normal functioning.

Figure 8.6: The seesaw of life—the art of finding balance

How we approach life and seek balance should mirror the innate ability our bodies possess. We often overlook how intelligent our bodies are, taking for granted the automatic processes that occur every second of the day. Our bodies are constantly striving for homeostasis, and we should aim to achieve the same. By being mindful of our state of being, we can take proactive steps to address the imbalances in our lives, allowing us to feel more centred.

In the midst of external chaos, remember to check in with yourself regularly, so you remain aware of the adjustments needed for your body and mind to return to balance. The goal is to become so in tune with your inner self that you know how to respond to these imbalances. During stressful periods, you might need to retreat more often than usual—this is perfectly acceptable. Allow yourself the permission to rest, reset, and recharge, whether it's for a day or even a week if you have a lot to process. A good rest day can enhance your productivity, enabling you to accomplish more and require less recovery time afterwards. By remaining fluid and attentive to your body and inner state, you can cultivate a dynamic form of balance as you continue to evolve.

As we continue to work at maintaining balance, we strengthen the foundation that supports clarity and intentional action. From this place of groundedness, we can begin to tap into our creative power to design a life that reflects not only our aspirations, but also the truth of who we are becoming.

9

Liberate

'Believe you can and you're halfway there.'
—Theodore Roosevelt

After exploring healing and balancing in previous chapters, you now understand the importance of these practices in creating the life you truly desire. Simply practising positive thinking or reciting affirmations is not enough to lift us from despair or break free from stagnation. The key reason for this is that we can only access our inner compass when we are calm and centred. This requires us to regulate our nervous system, which helps create a sense of safety and allows alignment to emerge naturally.

Healing is essential for uncovering the root causes of our limiting beliefs and our perceptions of the world. Balancing provides the foundation to remain centred and in harmony with the creative forces around us. It is important to recognize that this process is not linear but cyclical; we do not simply heal once and remain forever balanced. Instead, we move through continuous cycles of awareness, healing, balancing, and growth. As we resolve one layer of wounding, new insights emerge, revealing deeper patterns that also need attention. This cyclical journey spirals upwards, with each revolution bringing greater clarity, alignment, and an expanded capacity to create the life we envision.

Mindsets

Before we delve into the final stage of getting unstuck, let's take a look at three main mindsets you might be inhabiting:

- Living with resistance: the mindset of a victim
- Living with flow: the mindset of a victor
- Living with complete faith: the mindset of a manifestor

Living with resistance

One of the major obstacles to creating the life you desire and achieving your goals is your limiting belief system, the internal narrative that keeps you anchored in the past. Limiting beliefs prevent us from becoming who we are meant to be and, ultimately, from contributing to the world. As discussed earlier in the book, failing to recognize our limiting beliefs can lead to fear-based thought patterns, negative self-talk, and toxic cycles that reinforce these false beliefs. Without healing, reprogramming, and restructuring, it will be challenging to create a life that brings you joy and fulfilment.

In the art of manifestation, we have the power to rewrite our story. This does not mean we should ignore our past; rather, we can change our perception of it to gain a new perspective that facilitates growth and evolution. Each past event carries emotions, but when we detach ourselves from these emotions, our view of the story shifts from negative to more neutral. When this happens, our present and future are no longer dictated by our past, allowing us to finally feel unstuck.

When we live in a state of victimhood, we see ourselves as victims of our circumstances and avoid taking responsibility for our actions by blaming others or the situations around us. To break free from this mindset, we must begin to take ownership of our lives by making conscious choices and recognising our ability to grow through our past experiences. Shifting our mindset from victim to victor helps us transform the thought-emotion cycle from fear-based thinking to love-based thinking, one that opens us to joy, inspiration, growth, and deeper connection.

Fear is a stubborn energy because the belief that it protects us from harm is deeply rooted in the subconscious. As explained earlier in the book, we respond to perceived threats by entering survival mode, where fear takes over, a place where familiarity feels like safety. While stepping out of our comfort zone often brings discomfort, it is a necessary part of change. Staying within the known might feel certain and safe, but it limits what is possible.

This ingrained survival mechanism can hold us back from becoming who we are truly meant to be and over time, it can impact both our mental and physical well-being. So, the real question becomes: Who are we beneath the conditioning? What if the purpose of life isn't what we were taught to believe but something far more expansive, truthful, and aligned with who we really are? What is our purpose?

The difference between a purpose and a goal is that a goal offers temporary satisfaction that often fades as we adjust to our new circumstances, while purpose represents an evolving direction that feels true to your path and provides more lasting meaning. Goals, such as buying a house or owning a nice car, can provide a sense of security, stability, and achievement. However, many people still struggle to enjoy their accomplishments, because goals alone, especially material or status-driven ones, don't provide lasting fulfilment.

Purpose brings deeper meaning to our goals. It takes them to another level of commitment, becoming a steady source of motivation that fuels us with joy and passion. Sometimes, we follow a 'preconditioned purpose', the kind shaped by what we have been told matters: getting married, having children, making lots of money, or achieving social status. However, a life purpose is something entirely different. It comes from within. It's about what truly matters to you: what you care about, the values you live by, and how you want to contribute.

Life purpose isn't about how success looks on the outside; it's about what feels real and meaningful to you. It is shaped by your unique talents, your passions, and the way you want to share them with the world.

Living with flow

The state of 'flow', also known as creative flow, was introduced by positive psychologist Mihály Csíkszentmihályi as a way to achieve an internal state of creativity and happiness.[32] He described it as a mental state in which a person is completely present and engaged in a task. In the flow state, attention becomes highly focused, and awareness merges with action. Time may seem to slow down, or, for some, it feels timeless when they are performing at an optimal level. Learning how to enter the flow state can enhance our creativity and productivity, as well as align us with intuitive decision-making.

One key aspect of the flow state is that logical thinking is minimised, making every action feel effortless, as if it requires no conscious thought or analysis. To prepare ourselves for this state, we can practise our skills so thoroughly that they become automatic. This allows us to fully immerse ourselves in the flow state and perform at our best. As legendary NBA coach Phil Jackson describes in his book, *Eleven Rings: The Soul of Success*, players achieve what he calls a state where action flows naturally without conscious thought, through deliberate practice and mindfulness training.[33]

Similarly, professional chefs work in high-pressure environments where split-second decisions can make or break

---

[32] Mihály Csíkszentmihályi, *The Psychology of Optimal Experience* (HarperCollins, 2008).

[33] Phil Jackson and Hugh Delehanty, *Eleven Rings: The Soul of Success* (Penguin Press, 2013).

a service. They spend years mastering fundamental skills, such as knife work, timing, and seasoning, until these actions become second nature. This automatic mastery allows them to be fully present and in flow during intense service periods, where they must oversee multiple dishes while maintaining perfect standards.

Visualization functions in the same way. By mentally rehearsing and engaging both the mind and body as if the event is already happening, you can increase your chances of success. By repeatedly practising how you will perform, when the moment arrives, your mind and body will simply repeat a process they know inside and out.

Here are some tips for achieving a flow state:

- **Breathing exercises**
  Begin with breathing exercises to calm your mind and bring yourself into the present moment before starting a task. Once you are fully present, you can focus on the task at hand and strive to maintain that focus for as long as possible. The average duration for achieving flow is around thirty minutes to a few hours.
- **Clear goals and specific responses**
  Set clear goals and define specific responses. For example, in a tennis match, your main goal while serving is to maintain your advantage and secure a win, especially when you find yourself in an 'attacking' position, such as at the net.
- **Balancing challenge**
  According to Mihály Csíkszentmihályi, finding the right level of challenge is essential for staying in the flow. If a task is too easy, increase its difficulty; if it becomes overwhelming, enhance your skills to make it more manageable.
- **Distraction-free environment**
  Create an environment that is free from distractions. One of the primary modern distractions is our smartphones.

To achieve a flow state, it is crucial to silence your phone or remove it entirely from your immediate surroundings. This will help you immerse yourself fully in the task and boost your productivity and creativity.

- **Pursue your passions**
  It is more difficult to attain flow when engaging in tasks you dislike. If you find yourself in this situation, try to discover a way to make the task more enjoyable.

Understanding what brings us alive makes it easier to access the flow state. This journey begins with recognising what truly matters to us, what we care about, and what gives us a sense of purpose.

There are multiple methods and schools of thought that can help you achieve a flow state.

- **Finding your flow with ikigai**
  Ikigai is a Japanese concept that means 'a reason for being'. In recent years, it has gained popularity in the West as more people seek meaningful ways to live and work. At its heart, ikigai is about discovering what gives your life purpose and meaning—what motivates you to get up in the morning and makes life feel worthwhile. Ikigai is often found in small, everyday joys and meaningful moments rather than in grand life purposes or career choices. It is a way of life rather than a goal-setting framework.
  Does finding your ikigai mean your life will be completely stress-free? Not exactly. But research shows that living with purpose can help support the nervous system and reduce stress responses. When we lack clarity or feel disconnected from what brings us joy, it is easy to slip into overthinking or a victim mindset. Ikigai reminds us to stay focused on what truly matters and to see setbacks as part of the journey, rather than signs of failure.

When you are in alignment with your ikigai, things start to flow. You lose track of time, tasks feel lighter, and you are more present. Think of Roger Federer gliding across the tennis court, or Chris Martin lost in the music on stage—they are in their element, doing what they love, and it shows. That kind of presence and joy comes from living in flow and on purpose.

Remember, someone else's path isn't necessarily yours. A friend might thrive in a high-powered law career, but if public speaking or academic study isn't your strength, or if justice work doesn't inspire you, then chasing the same goal could leave you drained rather than fulfilled. Ikigai isn't about chasing success in the conventional sense. It's about honouring your own gifts and following what feels true to you.

So, what's your ikigai?

If you're feeling stuck or uncertain, take some time to reflect. Instead of trying to think your way out of confusion, recognise that clarity often comes from reconnecting with what truly inspires you. Consider the questions below as a guide to uncover what genuinely matters to you:

- What do you enjoy/love doing?
- What are you good at?
- What are your values?
- Who or what inspires you?
- What can you get paid for?
- What do you think the world needs and how can you contribute?

  Reflecting on these questions will help you map out a path that aligns with your true intentions, core values, and what you're here to do, leading to a greater sense of joy and fulfilment.

- **Living your truth with dharma**

The search for meaning and purpose is not unique to Japan. Cultures and spiritual traditions across the globe have long recognised the importance of living in alignment with who we truly are. While ikigai speaks to a practical balance between passion, skill, service, and sustainability, the Vedic tradition of India expresses a similar idea through the concept of *dharma*.

The meaning of dharma in Sanskrit is often translated as 'duty' or 'purpose', but its meaning runs much deeper. As Swami Chinmayananda, a renowned Indian spiritual teacher and founder of the Chinmaya Mission, explains that dharma is essentially 'the law of being'.[34] It is that which makes a thing what it is. Just as heat is the essential nature of fire and sweetness is the essential nature of sugar, dharma represents the fundamental essence of who we are.

In this light, dharma is not just about what you do but about who you are. It is your essence expressing itself through your actions. Life may still bring challenges, but when you live your dharma, there's a quiet, unwavering belief that you are on the right path. In Vedic philosophy, this inner radiance is known as tejas, a subtle fire or brilliance that reflects clarity, courage, and presence. It is the glow of someone rooted in purpose and not performing for the world but simply being themselves.

Just like ikigai, dharma invites you to honour your gifts, contribute meaningfully to the world, and live from a place of deep inner alignment. The magnetism you create doesn't come from striving or chasing, it comes from being in integrity with who you really are.

---

[34] Swami Chinmayananda, *The Holy Geeta* (Central Chinmaya Mission Trust, 1996).

- **Living with faith**

  Many of us have been conditioned to live a fear-based life. Traditional parenting and education systems tend to lean towards a reward and punishment framework. As a result, many of us grew up in environments largely influenced by fear, which was used to encourage good behaviour. Additionally, the media also plays a significant role in generating fear throughout our society. Fear-driven decision-making leaves no room for using imagination, let alone having faith during difficult times.

  Having faith involves cultivating deep trust, which may manifest as faith in God for some, or simply trusting one's own journey for others. It requires surrendering to the process, releasing worries about outcomes, and letting go of control.

  Letting go can be particularly challenging, as many people feel more secure when their lives are predictable. This fear of the unknown was especially pronounced during the Covid-19 pandemic, when uncertainty about how to protect ourselves made it difficult to maintain a sense of safety.

  The concept of accepting 'what is' requires us to trust completely that everything happens for a reason. When we view challenges as opportunities for growth, we can develop resilience and work towards a limitless life. A rejection can be seen as a redirection, shifting our mindset from a limited outlook to an unlimited one. By choosing to believe that endless opportunities lie ahead, rather than viewing situations as tragedies, we can keep ourselves moving forward.

  Perception has the power to make or break us. While we may not have control over unexpected circumstances in life, we can choose how we perceive and respond to them. When we trust the process, we don't waste our energy in self-pity or blame. Instead, we reserve all our valuable resources for creative thinking, which is vital to navigating our lives effectively.

Stepping into the flow requires us to embrace the unknown and trust that everything will ultimately work out for the best. This sense of certainty anchors us in our vision and fosters resilience, allowing us to navigate our journeys without letting outdated limiting beliefs sabotage our potential. With consistent practice, this mindset can become our default setting, requiring little effort to maintain. It becomes a part of who we are, knowing that whatever we set our minds to, will be realized, regardless of how or when it happens. This inner knowing helps us stay aligned, enabling us to seize opportunities for growth and expansion.

Creating Your New Reality

Everything in life, including our thoughts and emotions, carries an energetic quality. While the world appears solid, at the atomic level, everything is made up of energy in motion. In spiritual traditions, this energy is understood to vibrate at different frequencies, which many believe can influence how we feel and what we attract into our lives. The law of attraction is rooted in the idea that 'like attracts like'. When we embody the emotional state of what we desire, we begin to align ourselves with the experiences and opportunities that reflect that state. This aligns with what research in psychology and neuroscience shows that manifestation isn't just about thinking positively; it's about embodying the feeling of what we want and taking aligned action from a place of inner clarity and calm.

Thought = Map
Emotion = Magnet
Action = Momentum

Through healing, our thoughts and perspectives can be reframed, leading to a shift in how we feel about ourselves and our circumstances. This is how we change our vibration and elevate ourselves to become a vibrational magnet. Most people believe that their circumstances dictate their inner feelings; however, from a spiritual perspective, our external experiences are often a reflection of our internal state—this understanding is, at its core, the foundation of spirituality.

While it is true that external events can influence our emotions, but research (e.g., Viktor Frankl's work, mindfulness studies[35]) supports the idea that our inner state and perceptions significantly shape how we experience our circumstances. This is a dynamic interaction that reflects a spiritual truth increasingly validated by psychological insights.

When we shift our internal state, this influences how we perceive opportunities, the decisions we make, and the actions we take, which in turn shapes our lived experience. Viktor Frankl's work demonstrates that while we cannot always control our circumstances, we can choose our response to them, and this choice profoundly affects our path forward.

The process of creativity begins when we have a clear understanding of our purpose and desires, which allows us to take inspired actions. Many people may struggle to identify what they truly want due to societal pressures and expectations. A great way to address this is by listing the things that bring us joy. Recognizing the factors that contribute to our happiness and fulfilment can help guide us towards life paths that align with our hearts.

Personally, I discovered my path by embracing creativity, cherishing human connections, and finding fulfilment in facilitating healing and personal growth in others. These realizations have led me to a joyful and fulfilling life where work feels like a

[35] Viktor E. Frankl, *Man's Search for Meaning* (Beacon Press, 2006).

passion rather than a chore. This, I believe, is a clear indication that one has found their true purpose in life.

The Power of Imagination

All humans possess a unique gift known as imagination. The extent to which this imagination develops varies based on each individual's childhood learning experiences. Regardless of how imaginative you believe you are, how often do you use your imagination for creation? Do you take charge and use your imagination to design the life you desire, or do you allow life to unfold around you while your imagination remains underutilized?

Many people tend to focus their imaginative power on things they cannot change or control. For instance, they often replay past events, thinking about what they could have done differently, or they worry about potential future scenarios that may never come to pass. This habit usually centres on feelings of lack, such as: What if I don't have enough savings for retirement? What if I lose my job and end up homeless? What if this project doesn't succeed, and I lose all my investment money?

Negative thought patterns can consume a significant amount of our mental energy, placing us in a low vibrational state and keeping us in survival mode. When fear dictates our actions, it hinders our ability to access our creativity and inner wisdom. As mentioned previously, we can only tap into our intuition when we are not in a reactive state. To connect with this inner guidance, we must move out of survival mode by mastering our minds and emotions. It is only by turning our awareness inwards that we can hear our inner whispers and align our mind, body, and spirit.

When we are no longer driven by fear, we can channel all our energy towards creating our future while acknowledging and appreciating every single moment that we experience in the present.

Imagine a life filled with joy, love, and abundance. Think about the people you want to surround yourself with. Consider how it would feel to wake up each morning to a brand-new day, full of magical moments and new opportunities.

When you become aware of how you use your imagination, you can consciously shift from a fear-based mindset to a fearless one. A fearless imagination knows no limits. You can dream as big as you dare, free from rules and boundaries, allowing your mind to wander freely. Dream until you can feel emotions running through your body, excitement pulsating in your veins, and joy keeping your heart full.

Mastering the Art of Visualization

In the liberate toolkit you'll find later in the chapter, I will share techniques for rehearsing through visualization, which can help you use your imagination to create your vision. The purpose of rehearsing our desired vision is to train the brain to become familiar with what is unfamiliar, specifically, a vision that is entirely new and different from anything you have experienced in the past. This practice helps eliminate any limiting beliefs that may hinder our progress and builds trust in our vision.

As mentioned earlier in the book, our brain's primary function is to scan for danger and find the most efficient way to achieve an outcome. To reprogramme our system and change the way we think, feel, and behave, we must consciously reframe our thought patterns and mindsets. Studies in motor imagery and mental practice have shown that visualization activates many of the same neural circuits used during actual physical performance. By rehearsing what we desire, whether it is a new project or career, it is crucial to ensure that we are telling the brain that this is exactly what we want. When the brain becomes familiar with new beliefs and reality, our lives can become limitless, allowing us to courageously face any challenges that arise.

Imprinting the subconscious mind requires repetition and the instilling of positive emotions, a finding supported by research on emotional memory consolidation in the amygdala. While the exact percentage is debated, cognitive scientists estimate that between 90–95 per cent of our mental processes occur below conscious awareness, making it crucial to be completely aware of what we are imprinting onto the subconscious mind.

Our Emotional State Matters

By now, you would have a better understanding of how our emotions have a huge impact on how we experience life. When we honour and accept our emotions and use them as tools for healing, we are in a much better position to self-regulate and harness positive emotions to set intentions for our future. In his book, *Mind Magic*, James R. Doty, explains why positive emotions are important: 'Positive emotions activate the reward systems of our brains and therefore keep our inner compass set towards our intention. They also help us to free ourselves from the prison of old patterns created in our environment and prior actions.' [36]

He further explains that how well we visualize our intention can directly influence the emotions we experience, which strengthens the message we send to the brain to place more focus on the intention to make it happen.

In theory, this all sounds pretty straightforward, but practising it in real life is a lot more complex. There are some key factors that may affect your power of manifestation. To harness our innate

[36] James R. Doty, *Mind Magic: The Neuroscience of Manifestation and How It Changes Everything* (Penguin Publishing Group, 2024).

creative power, we need to raise our self-awareness and ensure we remain in the creative flow of life.

Here are some common roadblocks to manifestation:

- **When you are operating with a scarcity mindset**
  A scarcity mindset is a fear-based belief that there is not enough of what you want to achieve or obtain. Our limiting beliefs hold us captive in scarcity because they shape how we interpret challenges and opportunities, allowing negative thoughts to dominate our daily lives. The sense of lack is part of the limiting paradigm that prevents us from taking risks and overcoming challenges. One of the most effective ways to shift from a scarcity mindset to one of abundance is to practice gratitude daily. When we express gratitude for everything we have in the present moment, we open ourselves to receiving more positivity in our lives. Our emotional state shifts from lower states, such as fear and anxiety, to higher ones, such as joy and appreciation. While this shift isn't always instant, consistent gratitude practice has been shown to increase emotional resilience and help rewire our mindset over time.

- **When your energy and intentions clash**
  When you want to manifest a positive outcome, your energy must align with that reality to set things in motion. Let's say you are in a low vibrational state, meaning you are experiencing emotions like hopelessness, fear, or self-doubt. The reality you begin to experience will often mirror that emotional landscape, because our mindset influences the decisions we make and the people we attract. The art of manifestation calls us to elevate our internal state so that it becomes more supportive of what we want to bring into our lives.

If you want to start a new business but spend most of your energy replaying the betrayal from a past partnership, it becomes difficult to trust others or spot helpful opportunities. If you want a healthy, mutual relationship but remain emotionally stuck in resentment over past heartbreaks, those unprocessed emotions may unconsciously attract similar patterns. This is why healing is essential in the process of getting unstuck. We must learn to release the past and be fully present in the now, only then can we rewrite the story of our future.

The truth is, our patterns and behaviours reveal our inner beliefs. No matter how many times you script the life you want to create, if you still believe deep down that you are unworthy of love or success, it's likely that your reality won't shift. This mismatch occurs because the energy you are projecting into the world (through your thoughts, emotions, and behaviours) conflicts with the life you are trying to create. Healing and personal growth are not about forcing positivity; they are about transforming what we believe at the core.

Our subconscious beliefs will continue to influence our choices, reactions, and relationships until we address the root of those limiting stories. When we begin to notice the gap between what we consciously want and what we subconsciously believe we deserve, we gain the power to shift. And in that alignment between desire, belief, and action, new possibilities begin to emerge.

- **The inability to let go of control**

  When we set goals for ourselves, it is natural to feel anxious about how we will achieve them. However, if we focus too much on the specific ways we want things to happen, we risk missing out on unexpected opportunities. Furthermore, the anxiety of not having control can lead to even more stress when things don't go as planned. The key to successful manifestation is to establish an intention for the future we want while maintaining our focus on that vision. At the same time, it is important to let go of the need to dictate how it will unfold, including the expected outcomes and timing. Essentially, we should approach the creative process with joy and gratitude, which can cultivate a positive mindset and lead to desirable outcomes. As we do this, we often become more attuned to opportunities and connections that might otherwise go unnoticed.

We may find ourselves in the right place at the right time and meet people who can help us achieve our dreams. It is important to be aware of these signs and use them to guide us towards our ultimate destination by taking inspired actions. This is when we must trust our inner voice that gives us a nudge to do or say something, or to meet someone. Our intuition can help us navigate, provided we take the time to quiet our minds and listen periodically.

I like to use the phrase 'follow the breadcrumbs' to explain how to follow synchronicities for inspired actions. It's about noticing the subtle hints life gives us, such as seeing repeated numbers, encountering random opportunities, or recognising recurring themes. These are our breadcrumbs. As we pay attention to them, we begin to see patterns and make choices that feel right, even if we can't always explain why. Each small decision or action, guided by these intuitive nudges can shape our path. The more we follow these breadcrumbs, the more we tend to notice. It's a personal journey of learning to balance logic with a deeper sense of knowing. Just like everything in life, it's a constant balancing act.

When practising manifestation, we must bear in mind that things may not happen exactly as we wish. While setting intentions is crucial, we shouldn't let our desires prevent us from enjoying the journey. Being grateful in the present moment signals to our brain that positive things are already happening and that more good things can come our way. This helps elevate our energy, making us a magnet for positivity. On the other hand, if we are constantly pursuing future desires, our energy may become drained, leaving little for the present. After all, life is meant to be lived fully and not wasted chasing it away. Sometimes we just need to pause, take a breath, and really notice what is already here.

- **The lack of trust**
  When we set an intention, we must believe in our ability to turn it into reality. This belief helps us be open to receiving what we desire, as it activates our potential to recognize and respond to opportunities. Trusting in ourselves and the possibility of a better life is key to expanding what we believe is possible for us. Without confidence in our abilities, our intentions can easily become mere wishful thinking!

  It's easy to get caught up in worrying about the unknown and feeling powerless to shape our future. Remember that what you wish for may not necessarily turn out the way you expect, but this is usually for a good reason. When redirected, it's important to understand that what you want may not be what you need. Ultimately, everything tends to work out for the best. Maintaining trust in the face of challenges requires constant effort, but choosing to believe that things will work out can lead to positive outcomes.

When we trust that we are the creators of our lives and recognize that we all possess the power to shape our experiences, our mindsets transition from fixed to growth. Our emotions shift from despair to hope, and our thoughts move from limiting to liberating, enabling us to take appropriate actions when opportunities arise. Trust can eliminate our fears and is the quickest way to get us back on track, allowing us to move beyond the small details that keep us stuck in a rut. When our thoughts, emotions, and actions are aligned, we maximize our ability to create meaningful change in our lives.

- **When old patterns keep you stuck**

  One of the key practices in the pursuit of freedom is cultivating self-awareness through meditation and mindful practices. As you strengthen this awareness, it becomes easier to recognize and decode the patterns in your life. Many of these behaviours can be traced back to coping mechanisms formed in childhood, ways you learned to protect yourself or feel safe in response to your environment.

  For instance, one of my clients grew up in a household filled with disharmony, where tension and conflict were the norm. As a child, this made her feel unsafe, so she learned to avoid confrontation at all costs. Over time, this survival strategy became second nature. She steered clear of conflicts, uncomfortable conversations, or anything that felt like it might lead to a 'danger zone'. However, in doing so, she gradually lost her voice, suppressing her true feelings and disconnecting from her authentic self. Her thoughts, emotions, and actions were no longer aligned, and this misalignment left her feeling stuck, overwhelmed, and emotionally drained.

Despite her efforts to create vision boards, set intentions, or plan for the future she wanted, nothing seemed to change. She repeatedly asked herself why all her efforts weren't resulting in real transformation. The truth was that until she addressed the inner patterns, she remained unconsciously bound to her past, continually replaying the same coping strategies that no longer served her and confirming her feelings of being unsafe.

This type of avoidant behaviour is common for so many of us who fear rocking the boat, believing it's more important to be liked and accepted by others than to honour our own values and integrity. What once kept us safe can eventually become the very thing that holds us back.

By identifying and understanding these behaviours, we begin to loosen their grip and break the pattern. So, the next time you hit a roadblock and feel like your reality cannot change, pause and reflect: What pattern might be playing out here?

Rewire ➡ Reframe ➡ Realign

With compassion and curiosity, you can begin to rewire, reframe and realign with who you truly are, and find your way back into momentum.

- **Self-fulfilling prophecy**

  The concept of self-fulfilling prophecy reveals the profound impact our thoughts have on shaping our reality. It's as if our minds possess a hidden power to manifest the world we envision, whether those visions are positive or negative. When we expect certain outcomes, we unconsciously behave in ways that make those expectations come true. This highlights the powerful psychological process that influences our perceptions, decisions, and actions.

Our thoughts shape our future experiences. They determine how we interpret events, influence our emotional responses, and guide our choices. When we hold limiting beliefs about ourselves, we unknowingly create obstacles to our success. When we embrace empowering thoughts, we open doors to new opportunities.

Consider how this plays out in your daily life. If you believe you are capable of achieving a goal, you are more likely to persist in the face of challenges, seek help, and take calculated risks. Your actions, driven by your positive belief, increase the likelihood of success. If you doubt your abilities, you might avoid taking necessary steps, overlook opportunities, or give up when things get difficult.

By understanding how our thoughts shape our reality, we gain a powerful tool for personal transformation. We can consciously choose to cultivate thoughts that align with the life we want to create. This doesn't mean ignoring challenges or living in denial. Instead, it's about framing our experiences in ways that empower us rather than limit us.

Harnessing the power of self-fulfilling prophecy requires more than just positive thinking. It involves a deeper shift in our core beliefs about ourselves and the world. As we align our thoughts with our desired reality, we naturally adjust our actions and responses. By embracing empowering thoughts, we can tap into our innate potential to shape our lives. In doing so, we are not just passively hoping for a better future; we are actively participating in the creative process.

Embracing Change with Acceptance

When our lives are undergoing a major reset and renewal, we often notice that certain aspects naturally come to an end, whether or not we are prepared for it. There are moments when it feels as though things are being stripped away from us, making us fearful of the unknown and longing for security. Embracing change and stepping out of our comfort zones requires closing certain chapters to welcome new beginnings. While understanding this concept is straightforward, navigating the actual experience presents a unique set of challenges and emotions.

'Why me?' is the question I hear most from clients facing turbulent transitions. Many express feelings of frustration, stating, 'No matter how hard I try, everything keeps falling apart.' When we ask, 'Why me?' we unintentionally give away our power by framing life as something that happens to us rather than for us. This perspective denies our ability to influence how we feel about situations or what positive changes we can make.[37]

If someone chooses to leave your life without giving you a chance to make amends, accept and honour their decision. If you experience unexpected job loss without a valid reason, acknowledge it and move forward. The path to realignment lies in feeling our emotions fully without getting stuck in them. Emotions are meant to help us identify our triggers rather than ruminating endlessly on what we cannot change, which can keep us trapped in cycles of suffering. Instead, we should use our emotions as guides to identify areas in need of healing and shift our focus to reframing our thoughts and taking constructive action.

I'll be honest: having gone through many changes in the past couple of years has required courage, resilience, and complete faith to push through. I won't sugarcoat the process—the transition

---

[37] There's a tapping exercise to confront this feeling of 'Why me?' on pages 201 of this book.

period can be challenging. However, when we understand that this transition is only temporary and choose to trust that it may be creating space for new opportunities, we begin to accept what is. This acceptance helps us take a quantum leap into our new narrative and paradigm.

Acceptance is the key that unlocks the door to a new reality. When we embrace what is, rather than resist it, we open ourselves to the possibilities of what could be. This shift in perspective paves the way for transformative change and personal evolution. By accepting our current circumstances and challenges, we create a solid foundation from which we can launch ourselves into new experiences.

Accepting our reality doesn't mean giving up on change or settling for less than we desire. Rather, it means acknowledging where we are right now, without judgement or resistance. From this place of acceptance, we can respond to challenges with clarity and purpose, recognize opportunities we might have otherwise missed, and cultivate the resilience needed to navigate uncertainty. When we let go of our resistance and embrace acceptance, we free ourselves from the cycle of stuckness. We create space for new perspectives and solutions to emerge. By embracing what is, we unlock the potential of what could be, setting the stage for profound and lasting transformation in our lives.

The Importance of Alignment to Stay in the Flow

Gautama Buddha once said, 'Nothing can harm you as much as your own thoughts unguarded.' To stay in the flow and continue evolving into the best versions of ourselves, it is essential to remain dedicated to aligning our thoughts, emotions, and actions. When everything is aligned, challenges transform into opportunities, setbacks become signals for adjustment and improvement, and uncertainties reveal possibilities for new beginnings. Without resistance, we can navigate life's circumstances in a thriving state, allowing for inspired actions to take place rather than fear-driven reactions.

In order to thrive, we must stay attuned to our inner alignment, where our thoughts, emotions, and actions are in harmony and guided by our core values. This awareness prepares us to face whatever lies ahead from a place of clarity and trust.

Tennis serves as a perfect analogy for this concept. In tennis, to maintain flow, players must consistently return to the 'ready' position after each shot. This positioning ensures they're prepared for any incoming ball. When players fail to maintain readiness and effective positioning, they struggle to execute good shots and often fall into a defensive mode.

Life follows a similar pattern. To successfully navigate challenges, we must position ourselves mentally and emotionally, ensuring we are in the best state to face whatever comes next. Just as a well-positioned tennis player can respond effectively to any shot, a well-prepared individual can better handle life's unpredictable nature.

Alignment ➡ Positioning ➡ Respond

It is important to stay in alignment and respond to synchronicities with self-awareness. By consciously aligning our thoughts, emotions, and actions, much like a tennis player aligns their body on the court, we can respond to life's challenges from a position of readiness rather than reaction. This approach allows us to play the game of life with greater skill, adaptability, and ultimately, success.

Misalignment example

Belief: 'I'm not good enough.'
Thought: 'I won't be able to tackle this problem. I'm just not smart enough.'

Feeling: Unmotivated and uninspired.
Action: Inaction and procrastination.

Alignment example

Belief: 'I'm good enough.'
Thought: 'This task is tough, but I know I can do this.
I've got this.'
Feeling: Motivated and inspired.
Action: Upgrade skills and knowledge to tackle the problem.

When we neglect our alignment, we become more scattered and less focused. Feeling scattered and unfocused is a common experience for those who struggle to find their centre, where they feel safe and fully supported. When we don't feel safe, it can lead to self-defeating thoughts and cause us to react impulsively instead of responding thoughtfully to situations. Staying in alignment helps us gather the parts of ourselves that get pulled away by external factors. When we take time to retreat, withdraw our valuable energy, and go within, we instantly ground and centre ourselves, allowing us to make better decisions.

Living in alignment: a daily practice

At the end of 2024, everything shifted for me. Not in that dramatic, life-changing moment you see in movies, but in that subtle yet profound way that only happens when you finally understand something deep within your soul. After an intense period of self-reflection, acceptance and release, I discovered one simple truth that would become my daily motto: to practise staying in alignment.

When we are aligned, our minds settle into a state of unwavering focus, our bodies naturally relax, and we experience a heightened awareness that anchors us firmly in our present reality. This isn't just another mindfulness concept, it's a tangible state of being where we are completely tuned into life's subtle frequencies.

The beauty of living in alignment is how it transforms our relationship with gratitude. Instead of treating gratitude as another item on our self-improvement checklist, we naturally come to appreciate the wonderful things that appear in our lives, both big and small. This isn't forced positivity; it is a genuine recognition of life's magic unfolding before us.

But here's what most people don't understand about alignment: it's not a destination or a goal to be achieved. You can't simply tick it off your list and move on. It is a dynamic state that requires constant attention and adjustment. Some days, we need to slow down and ground ourselves. Other days, we need to ride the wave of momentum when we find our 'sweet spot'. The key is to regularly check in with ourselves, listening to what our bodies and minds tell us about our needs in each moment.

This practice of staying aligned has become my daily mission. It enables me to connect to my truth and remain open to life's infinite possibilities. When we are aligned, we naturally believe in the magic that makes life an extraordinary adventure.

Consider this: how often do we go through our days on autopilot, disconnected from our inner compass? We get caught up in the doing, the achieving, the endless cycle of goals and expectations. However, alignment brings us back to our centre, back to that space where we can truly feel what is right for us, the inner knowing.

The work of staying aligned isn't always easy. Like any meaningful practice, it requires dedication and presence. But unlike the rigid self-improvement routines we often force ourselves to follow, this practice flows naturally from a place of self-awareness. It's about continuously returning to ourselves, checking in with our inner knowing, and adjusting our course when needed.

This simple realization has completely transformed how I move through life. Instead of pushing against the current, I have learned to flow with it while staying true to my inner guidance. In this flow state, I have discovered that life has a way of surprising us with exactly what we need, exactly when we need it.

The Inner Conflict: When Head and Heart Are Out of Sync

One of the most disorienting experiences is the inner conflict that arises when your mind knows one thing, but your emotional body believes another. You might logically understand that you are no longer in the same situation, that you have done the work, and that you are safe now. Yet, your body keeps reacting as though the threat is still present. This is because your thinking brain (prefrontal cortex) may recognize safety, but your emotional brain (amygdala and limbic system) still detects danger. You may feel your chest tightening, your breath shortening, and your thoughts spiralling. Despite all the self-awareness you have gained, you find yourself falling back into old patterns again. This doesn't mean you are regressing; this is your body remembering.

What I refer to here as the emotional body includes the felt sense of unresolved emotions, often experienced in the heart, breath, or gut, that lingers even when the logical mind has moved on. It's part of what trauma expert Dr Bessel van der Kolk describes when he says that the body keeps the score; these imprints live in our nervous system, not just in our thoughts.

Past memories don't just exist in the mind; this is especially true for memories associated with pain, fear, shame, or rejection. These emotional imprints can live in the nervous system, the muscles, and what some describe as the energetic field. When your emotional body takes control, you are not responding to life as it is; instead, you are reacting based on who you needed to be in the past to feel safe, accepted, or loved.

This explains why we can know what to do yet still struggle to do it. We may sabotage ourselves, procrastinate, shut down, or over-function. This usually indicates that we haven't quite fully integrated our experiences—the mind may have updated, but the emotional body hasn't caught up.

This is where my 'inner alignment method', detailed later in the chapter, is particularly useful. This method was born from years of personal trial, spiritual study, and working with clients who consistently hit the same wall despite doing 'all the right things'. It combines breath and body awareness, energy balancing, visualization, and embodied presence to help you come back to your centre where clarity can be gained.

Clarity alone isn't the goal. What we're really looking for is integration, where your head and heart begin speaking the same language. This is what allows real transformation to take place.

How Integration Happens

Integration happens when your thoughts and emotions come into alignment. You are no longer pulled between what you 'should' believe and what you actually feel. Instead of dismissing your feelings, you honour them, meet them with curiosity, and gently rewire them with new truths. Here's what the integration process can look like:

- **Recognize the disconnect**
  Start by noticing when you are out of alignment. You might be saying, 'I've moved on,' but still feel tense, anxious, or heavy. That's your emotional body signalling there's still something unprocessed. Naming this gap is the first act of integration.
- **Regulate the nervous system**
  When your body is dysregulated, you can't access intuitive thinking. Using tools like EFT tapping, breathwork, or

grounding practices, you soothe the nervous system so your body can feel safe enough to release old protective mechanisms.

- **Access the emotional body**
  The emotional body doesn't respond to logic, it responds to presence. The inner alignment method helps you gently connect with stored emotions and unresolved memories—not to relive them, but to finally release them.
- **Rewire through felt experience**
  You can't just repeat affirmations and hope they stick. For new beliefs to take root, you have to feel their truth in your body. The shift happens when you can say, 'I am safe now,' and your whole system agrees. That's when transformation becomes sustainable.

Integration is not about becoming someone new, it's about remembering who you have always been—beneath the armour, the roles, the trauma responses. It's about calling back the parts of you that got left behind and making space for them to return. This is the real work of getting unstuck.

When your emotional body no longer has to protect you from a past that no longer exists, and when your mind no longer has to carry the burden of suppressing those emotions, you are free. Not because life is perfect, but because you are no longer at war within yourself. To support this freedom, staying grounded through simple daily practices becomes essential. Regulating the nervous system through breathwork, movement, or quiet moments of reflection helps your body feel safe enough to keep expanding, rather than bracing for the worst. It's this ongoing sense of safety that allows you to live, create, and connect with more ease.

UNSTUCK Toolbox for Liberate

Staying in alignment

Here are some common feelings when there's a misalignment:

- Offbeat
- Reactive
- Restless
- Indecisive
- Ungrounded
- Scatter-minded (all over the place)
- Overwhelmed
- Overly sensitive

To address this misalignment and correct it, there are several methods you can employ to help you get back into alignment—some of which are listed below.

1. Make it a habit to meditate daily to clear your mind and increase your awareness. It is in silence that we can hear our inner guidance, which might get drowned out by outside noise. With regular practice, this feeling of serenity becomes part of who we are, making us more attuned to our emotions and thoughts. Starting your day with meditation can help you maintain balance throughout the day.
2. Be mindful of your thoughts, especially the inner dialogue that you tend to repeat. Reframing your thoughts in chaotic situations can help you maintain a positive mindset and take necessary actions to create a constructive outcome.
3. Be aware of your emotions. Develop a daily practice to check in with your bodily sensations, where you store stress and tension. Follow this by understanding where the

emotions originate from and how you can dissolve them by reducing emotional intensity and reframing your thoughts with EFT tapping.

4. Raise your vibration by practising gratitude and bringing joy into your daily life. Joy is essential for restoring overall well-being and harmony. The more chaotic life may seem, the more important it becomes to dedicate time to activities that nurture your inner happiness.

Creative visualization

Visualization is a mental exercise that is gaining popularity among many successful entrepreneurs and athletes as a way to prepare mentally for their goals. Professional tennis players, like Novak Djokovic, use visualization as an essential part of their preparation before each match. By doing this, they prime their minds to experience victory, allowing their bodies to respond with greater ease and confidence. When we align ourselves with the future we desire, we enhance our chances of success and begin creating the life we truly want.

Scripting is an intentional writing exercise for visualization, a mental rehearsal for the future you want to create. This is a great exercise for writing down your aspirations and imagining what it would feel like to live your dream life. This practice provides clarity and purpose, aligning you with your vision.

The key to scripting is to come from a place of gratitude and abundance rather than lack. Instead of saying, 'I need a new job,' try saying, 'I am grateful for the job I have right now. I am ready for something even better and welcome the new opportunities that come my way as I navigate my professional life.' Be specific about what you want to manifest but also keep an open mind so that anything better than your initial wishes can flow into your life.

Renowned hypnotherapist and motivational speaker Marisa Peer explains how we can use the power of words to change our reality.[38] When we pay attention to the words we use in creating a new reality, we must remain in a positive mindset and truly believe in our capability to achieve our desired results. In addition to scripting in the present tense (as if what you're asking for is already happening), it's important to engage all five senses when describing your vision. Emotion plays a significant role in this practice.

When scripting the vision you are creating, it is essential to feel the emotions associated with future vision as if they are happening now. While some people refer to this as 'fake it till you make it', I find that phrase somewhat negative. Our minds are clever enough to know that we are only faking it because, deep down, we don't believe our dreams will come true. Instead, we want to feel and think like the version of ourselves who is already living in that new reality. By aligning our thoughts and emotions with what we are trying to create, we open ourselves to new possibilities and opportunities. Many people find that this alignment, whether you call it the law of attraction, manifestation, or simply focused intention, helps them move towards their desired outcomes.

Prompts: Scripting for visualization

Step 1: Take a couple of minutes to centre yourself so you are writing from a place of calmness. Close your eyes and focus on your breath for 5 to 10 minutes. Simply observe your breath without trying to change it. When you are ready, you can open your eyes and start writing.

Step 2: Get creative! Be specific about what you are creating for yourself in the present tense, as if it were already

[38] Marisa Peer, 'Why the Words You Say Matter | Marisa Peer,' posted on September 20, 2021, by Marisa Peer, YouTube, https://www.youtube.com/watch?v=Qmbhf5j76CE

happening. Imagine you are the screenwriter, director, and star of your dream life. You get to be as creative as you like and as bold as you can be.

Step 3: Write down your thoughts and emotions and try to visualize and experience the vision you are creating with your senses. What can you see? What can you hear? Feel the emotions in your body and believe that the thoughts you have are true, as if you are rehearsing for the role of the main character of your life.

Visualization exercise: Rehearsing for the main character role

Step 1: Read your script and imagine you are living your future life. Reread your script until you experience all the emotions that your future life creates for you. Marinate yourself in the feel-good vibes, and then let go completely, allowing space for things to unfold as they should.

Step 2: Visualize the movie of your dream life on a movie screen with your mind's eye. You can do this first thing in the morning before you start your day, or just before you drift off to sleep at night.

As most manifestation experts will tell you, it is important to be in emotional alignment with your goals, and to genuinely believe you have the ability to achieve them for your dreams to become reality. However, many of us encounter deeply ingrained limiting beliefs that can hold us back from pursuing our goals and desires.

This is where EFT tapping can support the process. Once you have written your script, you may start to hear your inner critic judging what you have written, which could lead you to stop believing in your power to make things happen for yourself. When this happens, simply tune in and ask yourself what emotions you are feeling. You may feel doubtful because you don't believe you are good enough. You may feel anxious that everything will fall apart and you will risk losing what you have. Write down these emotions for the following EFT script and start tapping.

Tapping for mindset shift

1. Read the script and take note of the emotions you feel while reading it.
   Example: *I am feeling anxious.*
2. Notice any limiting beliefs that arise.
   Example: I am not good enough.
3. What other statements can you make about the script?
   Example: This is wishful thinking. I am never this lucky.
4. Rate the intensity of your feelings on a scale of 0 to 10.
   Example: Intensity 8
5. Start tapping on these feelings. It is okay if you don't want to name the emotions; you can simply tap on 'these emotions'. The more specific you can be, the more effective the tapping will be for shifting the energy. Begin with the set-up statement on the karate chop point:
   - *Even though I'm feeling all these emotions right now, I deeply and completely accept myself.*
   - *Even though I have all these emotions that are surfacing right now, I'm giving myself permission to acknowledge and accept them. I deeply and completely honour my feelings.*

Round 1

Top of the head:

These emotions.

Eyebrow:

All this anxiety.

Side of the eye:

Feeling anxious.

Under the eye:

But it's okay. I am safe.

Under the nose:

All these feelings.

Chin point:

All these emotions [you can start naming them].

Collarbone:

I'm feeling the tightness in my body and the pressure on my shoulders.

Under the arm:

I'm choosing to acknowledge and release them.

Round 2

Top of the head:

I'm choosing to let go of what no longer serves me.

Eyebrow:

I'm choosing to let go of [state whatever comes up for you or repeat the emotions that you are feeling].

Side of the eye:

I'm choosing to relax.

Under the eye:

I'm letting it all go.

Under the nose:

I'm choosing to release [name the emotions].

Chin point:

Letting go.

Collarbone:

I acknowledge this self-doubt.

Under the arm:

And all the limiting beliefs that are holding me back.

Round 3

Top of the head:

I am choosing to release them all now.

Eyebrow:

I can figure things out as I go.

Side of the eye:

I can learn from every life experience.

Under the eye:

I am ready to take action.

Under the nose:

And trust that everything will work out just fine.

Chin point:

I am enough.

Collarbone:

I am worthy.

Under the arm:

I am safe.

Tap on heart space (thymus):

Releasing all these emotions in my mind and body so I can completely relax. All is well. I am safe.

Continue to tap until you feel completely relaxed, when you rate the intensity as zero. Then place your hands on your chest and seal the energy. Notice how you feel, observe any shifts in your body, enjoy the stillness, take a deep breath into your heart space and then breathe out while saying, 'Transform.'

Inner alignment method

The inner alignment method is a signature method I use to harmonize the mind, body, and energy system. This guided practice is designed to help you connect with your breath, tune into your body, and balance your energy centres (chakras).

From this state of calm awareness, we transition into gratitude and intentional visualization, planting seeds of creativity in the subconscious mind.

Step 1: Breath awareness—opening the practice

Prepare for the exercise by focusing on your breath. Make sure your spine is straight, your neck is relaxed, and your head is in a neutral position. Visualize an invisible string at the top of your head gently pulling you upwards towards the sky, allowing your spine to lengthen. Pull your shoulders back to open your heart space, then relax your shoulders.

Step 2: Body awareness—releasing tension

Allow yourself to fully relax. Gently scan your body from head to toe, paying attention to any areas of tension or tightness. Inhale deeply through your nose, then exhale through your mouth to let go of that tension. Repeat this process until you feel completely relaxed, then return your focus to your breath and observe your breathing pattern.

Step 3: Energy alignment—chakra visualization

Bring your awareness to each of the seven main energy centres in your body (chakras). Visualize the associated colours and qualities as you move from the base of your spine to the top of your head.

- **Root chakra (*muladhara*)—base of the spine**
  Visualisze a vibrant red light at the base of your spine. Feel grounded, safe, and supported.
- **Sacral chakra (*svadhisthana*)—lower abdomen, below the navel**
  Visualize a warm orange glow. Connect to creativity, pleasure, and emotional flow.
- **Solar plexus chakra (*manipura*)—upper abdomen, above the navel**

Visualize a bright yellow light. Feel your confidence, clarity, and personal power awaken.

- **Heart chakra (*anahata*)—centre of chest**
  Visualize a soft green light. Let compassion, love, and openness fill your heart.
- **Throat chakra (*vishuddha*)—throat**
  Visualize a clear blue light. Open your voice, expression, and inner truth.
- **Third eye chakra (*ajna*)—forehead**
  Visualize a deep indigo light. Activate your intuition and inner knowing.
- **Crown chakra (*sahasrara*)—top of head**
  Finally, visualize a radiant violet or white light. Connect to your higher consciousness and sense of unity.

Take a moment and imagine all the lights merging into a luminous white light that surrounds your entire body. Feel your energy aligned and flowing freely.

Step 4: Gratitude—opening to receive

Once you find yourself in a state of complete stillness, begin to think of five things for which you are grateful. This could be someone you love, your home, or a positive experience at work that you take pride in. Focus on these moments that bring a sense of gratitude. Pay attention to the emotions you experience and where you feel them in your body, such as joy in your heart or excitement in your hands.

Step 5: Intentional creation—visualize your desire

From this elevated state, plant the seed of what you wish to create. It could be launching a new business, purchasing your dream house, or planning a lovely family holiday. Create mental images and project them onto an imaginary movie screen. Visualize your desire as vividly as possible. Visualize the process: imagine the steps you would take to reach your goal. See yourself working, collaborating, and overcoming challenges. Engage your senses by imagining how achieving your goal would look, feel, sound, smell, and even taste. Immerse yourself in this scene. What do you see? What do you hear? What emotions arise?

Now, picture the moment of success. This might be the completion of your project, the celebration of your achievement, or the positive impact it has on others. Feel the joy, pride, and satisfaction radiating from you. Allow this feeling to wash over you, filling you with confidence and motivation.

Step 6: Closing—release and return

To conclude the practice, start by bringing your awareness back to your breath and then to your body. Take a deep inhalation, and as you exhale, let go of your attachment to the outcome and trust the process. Gently move your fingers and toes, and then the rest of your body. When you feel ready, slowly open your eyes.

Tapping for resistance to change—'Why me?'

1. Tune into the changes you have experienced recently.
2. Notice any emotions that are showing up and/or notable physical sensations.
   Examples: Frustration and anger, tightness in the throat and chest.
3. What is the repeated inner dialogue you keep noticing?
   Examples: 'Why me?', 'When is my life going to get better?'
4. Rate the intensity of these emotions or sensations from 0 to 10.
   Example: Intensity 6/10
   Start with the set-up statement on the karate chop point:
   - *Even though I feel overwhelmed by all the changes happening in my life, I choose to love and accept myself anyway.*

- *Even though I'm scared and frustrated, and nothing seems to be improving, I choose to honour these feelings.*
- *Even though I feel like I'm hitting one roadblock after another, I choose to love and accept myself exactly as I am.*
- *Even though part of me is angry, hurt, or just tired of it all, I choose to deeply and completely honour my feelings and allow myself space to process them anyway.*

Round 1

Top of the head:

Why is this happening to me?

Eyebrow:

Why does it feel like I'm always the one struggling?

Side of the eye:

Why me?

Under the eye:

Why does it feel like things just keep getting worse?

Under the nose:

Why do I keep hitting roadblocks?

Chin point:

Nothing seems to be getting better.

Collarbone:

Why do I feel so alone in this?

Under the arm:

I'm tired of feeling stuck.

Round 2

Top of the head:

It feels like it just sucks to be me right now.

Eyebrow:

This heaviness in my chest . . . this tightness in my throat.

Side of the eye:

I feel so frustrated and defeated.

Under the eye:

I feel so exhausted, I don't know if I have what it takes to get through this.

Under the nose:

Part of me just wants it to stop.

Chin point:

But I'm still here. I'm still showing up.

Collarbone:

So what if . . . something is trying to shift?

Under the arm:

What if I could begin to accept what I'm feeling?

Round 3

Top of the head:

What if I could honour these emotions instead of fighting them?

Eyebrow:

What if letting go of what no longer serves me creates space for something new?

Side of the eye:

What if this is to prepare me for something better?

Under the eye:

I choose to accept where I am right now.

Under the nose:

I choose to accept these changes, even if I don't understand them yet.

Chin point:

I choose to remain open to opportunities.

Collarbone:

I choose to honour my emotions and trust in the unfolding process.

Under the arm:

I am safe (Repeat 'I am safe' two or three times while tapping here.)

Tap on heart space (thymus):

I release these emotions from my mind and body now.
I trust myself to navigate whatever comes.
I allow myself to relax, to soften, and to return to stillness.
I am safe.

Rate the intensity of the emotions and physical sensations. Continue to tap on them until the intensity drops to zero. Then place your hands on your chest and seal the energy. Observe the energy shift, enjoy the stillness, take a deep breath into your heart space and then breathe out and say, 'Transform.'

Refocus and Realign

In this chapter, we have been exploring ways to manifest our desires. However, what happens when our desires become so intense that we lose sight of the present moment? Worse still, we may become impatient with the process and unknowingly create resistance to change by fixating on our desired outcomes. By loosening our grip on how we think things should manifest, we open ourselves up to possibilities that are beyond our imagination.

To dissolve feelings of urgency and desperation, we must take a broader perspective on our situation. This involves gaining a deeper understanding of why this fixation exists in the first place. For example, consider the desire for financial freedom. The essential question is: what truly lies at the heart of this desire? Is it about accumulating wealth, or is it about the freedom that financial security brings? Many of our desires lead us towards the concept of freedom. Let's shift our focus to this idea of freedom and use it to transform our mindset.

Begin by acknowledging all the freedom you currently enjoy. Here are several thought-provoking examples:

- *I am free to choose my emotional state from the moment I awaken.*
- *I am free to select nourishing or comforting food throughout my day.*
- *I am free to determine my relationship with technology and digital connection.*
- *I am free to express myself through my choice of clothing and appearance.*
- *I am free to honour my body through movement and rest as I see fit.*
- *I am free to cultivate relationships that uplift and inspire me.*
- *I am free to invest my precious time and energy in people and pursuits that truly matter.*

And the list goes on . . . you get the gist of it. The principle becomes clear as you reflect. By redirecting your awareness from the freedom you perceive as lacking to the abundant freedom already present in your life, you naturally align your mindset and emotional state with your desired outcome—freedom itself. Rather than fixating on scarcity thoughts like, 'I won't experience freedom until I earn a certain amount annually,' you embrace an abundance mindset that affirms you are ready to welcome even greater freedom into your life. This profound yet simple practice can instantly restore your alignment, much like expressing heartfelt gratitude for the blessings currently in your life.

Allow Things to Unfold While Working Towards Your Goals

Committing to daily mindfulness practices, processing our emotions, reframing our thoughts, and knowing how to realign ourselves during chaotic times can make life feel more effortless. By actively engaging in the present moment and being mindful of our inner balance, we create space for magic to happen.

The art of allowing life to unfold while steadily taking inspired action is a constant balancing act. Staying in alignment requires us to take time to pause and check in with our feelings about our current situation, finding peace within it. There's no need to rush, and no reason to worry if things are moving slowly. Remember, the 'sweet spot' is right at the centre. Any hint of imbalance is a cue for us to reflect on what adjustments we need to make in order to stay on track and be prepared for whatever comes next.

10

Framework Recap: Dancing with the Universe

In the get-unstuck journey, we start with healing to address the issues that have kept us feeling stuck. By regaining our balance and mastering our minds and emotions, we can step back into the creative flow of life. This process helps us cultivate self-love and fully accept who we truly are. Authenticity helps us break free from our masks and reveal our true essence, allowing us to share our gifts with the world.

When we align ourselves with our true calling and embrace the joy that is always available, we enter an elevated state of being. This state allows us to navigate life with an open heart and complete trust in ourselves and our journey. A life lived not controlled by fear is truly liberating. We always have the freedom to choose. Living courageously means focusing on what can be done in the present moment, trusting in our power to create change. This internal balance can only be achieved and maintained by you, requiring self-awareness and ongoing inner work as we respond to the unpredictable challenges and opportunities that life presents. In both cases, change is inevitable.

To fully liberate ourselves, we must have the courage to step into the unknown and create a new paradigm. We must cultivate mindfulness and become observers of our thoughts and emotions. Most importantly, we have to acknowledge that we are fully responsible for our actions, and we should use our own discernment to make decisions that align with our values and desires. As we rediscover our authenticity through healing, love, and acceptance, our lives become more purposeful and fulfilling, allowing us to follow our intuition rather than fear-based decisions.

When we trust our inner guidance, we learn to work with, not against, what is being placed on our path and respond fearlessly. Living without being controlled by fear means viewing every challenge as an opportunity for growth, not as a reason for despair. A fearless response empowers us to rise up to challenges, bounce back from setbacks, and maintain hope that the best is yet to come. We become the detectives of our own lives by connecting the dots, untangling the knots, and paving a smoother path ahead.

The way forward lies in creating space from our emotions so we can listen, with a calm mind, to the place where all our answers reside. When we understand and follow the mystical orchestration, those meaningful patterns and synchronicities in our life events, we can finally dance to the rhythm of the universe.

Onwards and Upwards

The UNSTUCK framework is a cyclical approach to self-mastery that provides key reference points: heal, balance, and liberate, to help you respond to life's unpredictability from a place of stillness and remain in the flow.

As the saying goes, life is like a rollercoaster ride, filled with ups and downs, highs and lows, but none of them last forever. In truth, we have the freedom to choose how we experience and respond to life's circumstances. With hindsight, there are always things we could have done better, but dwelling on the past does not propel us forward; it hinders our journey towards greatness.

Learning from past experiences and being accountable for our actions is what can free us from habitual patterns. While holding ourselves accountable is vital for personal growth, it is equally important to show ourselves love and compassion throughout this process, so we avoid falling into a cycle of self-criticism. Love and compassion are the ultimate antidotes to feeling stuck.

By establishing new habits that support our journey and maintain our focus, we can begin to embrace our unique talents and step into our full potential. Engaging in daily practices such as meditation to stay aligned, tapping to feel secure, practicing gratitude to elevate our mood, and participating in activities that bring us joy can lead to significant transformation. This shift in perspective nurtures our inner state of being. This is how we get unstuck.

It is important to remember that what may feel like a setback is actually an opportunity for a transformative period where we can reset and regroup. Breakdowns often lead to breakthroughs, and it is in the darkness that our inner flame can shine its brightest.

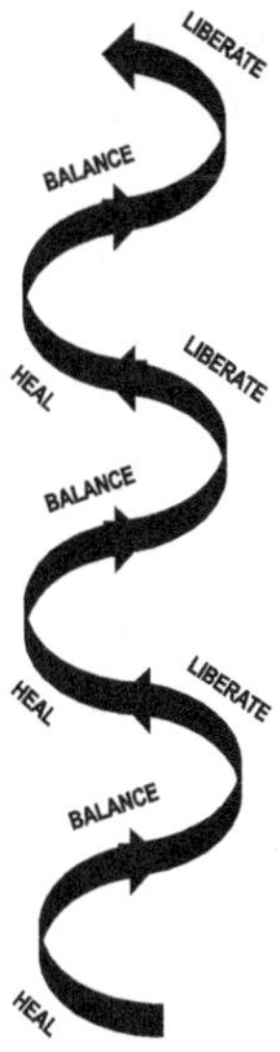

Figure 10.1: The cyclical nature of the UNSTUCK framework

This is the beginning of the UNSTUCK cycle—when our emotions illuminate what needs healing. From there, we reach a point of balance and gradually work our way towards liberation. Nothing in life is permanent, and change is the only constant we have. This very idea inspired the creation of this framework, which is as dynamic as life itself. When we let go of our need to control how things unfold and embrace uncertainty, it opens us up to unexpected blessings.

Final Note

This book offers an overview of how to get yourself unstuck. The UNSTUCK framework is a methodology you can adopt when facing challenging situations. There is no definitive starting or finishing point; instead, it is a cyclical model that you can refer to throughout your journey of self-mastery. While your awakening won't shield you from life's adversities and challenges, you can equip yourself with the awareness and practices suggested in this book to help you bounce back to your 'sweet spot'.

If you haven't started your healing journey yet, I hope this book will inspire you to take the first step, understanding that there is no shame in seeking the help and emotional support you need to live a better life. You are more than enough, and now is the time to let go of the misconceptions about yourself so you can live courageously. It is time to become unstuck.

Throughout this book, I have shared suggestions for healing and finding balance. The modalities and practices mentioned have worked exceptionally well for me. However, there are numerous healing and therapeutic methods available that can help you heal, find balance, and liberate yourself. Fear may be the only thing stopping you from embarking on this journey, but it will dissipate over time as you begin to reap the rewards of your efforts.

One of the biggest roadblocks I have overcome in my personal journey is the fear of judgement—the fear of how others perceive me. This subtle yet profound shift in mindset has allowed me to live authentically, speak my truth, and act in alignment with my heart and soul. Just as we get fit by working out in the gym to strengthen our bodies, we should invest in our mental health to remain mentally fit for as long as possible. Seeking a mentor or coach can help you achieve this.

The UNSTUCK framework is my most significant creation, empowering me to navigate through challenging circumstances with clarity and purpose. During periods of profound difficulty, this approach has consistently helped me to untangle limiting thought patterns and face each challenge from a fresh perspective. This framework guides individuals to reclaim their personal power by consciously choosing not to be governed by external circumstances. It encourages the creation of meaningful change by realigning one's inner landscape, which naturally manifests in the outer reality. This level of wholeness transforms us into authentic creators of our own experiences, allowing us to shape our narratives intentionally and on our own terms.

The healing continues as I navigate through this beautiful experience called life, one step at a time. My wish for you is to experience an awakening that frees you from emotional burdens, self-limiting beliefs, and societal expectations so you can reclaim your power and become the captain of your own ship.

Dada Vaswani, a world-renowned spiritual leader, once famously said, 'True success, true happiness lies in freedom and fulfillment.'

And freedom is our birthright.

References

Brown, Brené. *Daring Greatly: How the Courage to Be Vulnerable Transforms the Way We Live, Love, Parent, and Lead.* Penguin Publishing Group, 2012. eBook.

Brown, Brené. *The Gifts of Imperfection.* Simon and Schuster, 2022. eBook.

Chinmayananda, Swami. *The Holy Geeta.* Central Chinmaya Mission Trust, 1996.

Clear, James. *Atomic Habits: An Easy & Proven Way to Build Good Habits & Break Bad Ones.* Avery, 2018.

Covey, Stephen M. R. *Trust & Inspire: How Truly Great Leaders Unleash Greatness in Others*. Simon and Schuster, 2022.

Csíkszentmihályi, Mihály. *The Psychology of Optimal Experience.* HarperCollins, 2008.

Dandapani. *The Power of Unwavering Focus.* Penguin Publishing Group, 2022.

Demartini, John. *The Breakthrough Experience: A Revolutionary New Approach to Personal Transformation*. Hay House, 2009.

Doty, James R. *Mind Magic: The Neuroscience of Manifestation and How It Changes Everything*. Penguin Publishing Group, 2024.

Eremia, Cristina. 'SCIENCE OF THE HEART: Exploring the Role of the Heart in Human Performance HEARTMATH,' n.d.

Frankl, Viktor E. *Man's Search for Meaning*. Beacon Press, 2006.

Goleman, Daniel. *Emotional Intelligence: Why It Can Matter More Than IQ*. Bloomsbury, 2009. eBook.

Hawkins, David R., *Letting Go: The Pathway of Surrender*. Hay House, 2018.

Hay, Louise. *You Can Heal Your Life*. Hay House,1984.

HeartMath Institute. 'Science of the Heart: Exploring the Role of the Heart in Human Performance.' Research. https://www.heartmath.org/research/science-of-the-heart/energetic-communication/

Jackson, Phil and Hugh Delehanty. *Eleven Rings: The Soul of Success*. Penguin Press, 2013.

Judith, Anodea. *Wheels of Life: A User's Guide to the Chakra System*. Llewellyn Publications, 2002.

Kolk, Bessel van der. *The Body Keeps the Score: Brain, Mind, and Body in the Healing of Trauma*. Penguin Publishing Group, 2014.

Kolk, Bessel van der. 'What is trauma? The author of "The Body Keeps the Score" explains | Bessel van der Kolk | Big Think.' Posted on September 17, 2021, by Big Think. YouTube. https://www.youtube.com/watch?v=BJfmfkDQb14

Lee, Bruce and John Little, dir. *Bruce Lee: A Warrior's Journey*. Warner Home Video, 2000.

Lipton, Bruce H. *The Biology of Belief: Unleashing the Power of Consciousness, Matter and Miracles*. ReadHowYouWant, 2010.

Lipton, Bruce H. '95 % Of The Day, You Are Not Operating From The Conscious Mind - Bruce Lipton.' Posted on August 26, 2021, by Success Archive. YouTube. https://www.youtube.com/watch?v=ZjZvtrKNvzU

Maté, Gabor. *When the Body Says No: The Cost of Hidden Stress*. Wiley, 2011. eBook.

Peer, Marisa. 'Why the Words You Say Matter | Marisa Peer.' Posted on September 20, 2021, by Marisa Peer. YouTube. https://www.youtube.com/watch?v=Qmbhf5j76CE

Rumi, Jalal ad-Din Muhammad. *The Essential Rumi.* Translated by Coleman Barks. HarperCollins Publishers, 1995.

Stapleton, Peta. 'The Latest Science of Clinical EFT Tapping.' Virtual lecture. Posted on June 19, 2023, by Dr Peta Stapleton. YouTube. https://youtu.be/GMa6Dv4OUrc

Acknowledgements

This book wouldn't exist without the people who believed in it, and in me.

My family has been my foundation. My dad, for his quiet, unshakeable belief in me. Uncle Bing, for inspiring me to create fearlessly. My mum, for her unwavering support through every triumph and struggle. She never gave up on me, even when I couldn't see the way forward myself. And to my daughter Amelia, my biggest cheerleader, my source of joy, and the one who brightens even my darkest days. Your fun-loving spirit has been a gift throughout this journey.

To Toby, for the support you gave during our years together, and for the greatest gift—our daughter Amelia.

To the friends I trust most—you know who you are. The ones who've shown up again and again, held space for the messy bits, celebrated every win, and reminded me I'm never doing this alone. Thank you for being there.

Piyaji has been my spiritual mentor since 2011, teaching me what it means to live a truly heart-led life. She has a gift for reflecting back what I already know deep down but choose to ignore, and her honest yet compassionate guidance always brings me back to centre. When life turned upside down in 2022 and I returned to her classes after a two-year absence, she and my classmates welcomed me with open arms, providing the safe space I needed to heal and grow.

Tamara and Peter Donn generously shared their Emotional Freedom Technique expertise with me, and I never expected the training itself would become such a pivotal part of my healing journey. Some of my most transformative breakthroughs happened during tapping sessions with Tamara, and I'm deeply appreciative that she held space for those moments. She also kindly proofread the EFT sections of this book and provided invaluable feedback. If you're curious about learning EFT, check out their website https://efttrainingcentre.com

Jerica Liew and Nathanael Lim from KOVA Branding have been instrumental in bringing UNSTUCK to life visually. Jerica designed the logo and book cover, and both of them believed in this framework from the very beginning. Their creative vision and feedback on the branding have been invaluable.

My thanks to Tamsin Bradshaw for helping refine my book proposal, and to Jo Salim for capturing my promotional photos. Your support throughout this journey has meant so much.

I'm deeply thankful to the Penguin Publishing Group Southeast Asia team, especially Nora, for believing in this book from the start and championing it every step of the way.